# FROM SEED TO CEDAR

Nurturing the Spiritual Needs in Children

A Guide for Muslim Families

# FROM SEED TO CEDAR

Nurturing the Spiritual Needs in Children

M. Fethullah Gülen

New Jersey

Copyright © 2014 by Tughra Books

17 16 15 14     2 3 4 5

Originally published in Turkish as *Çekirdekten Çınara* in 2002

Translated by Dr. Ali Köse and Korkut Altay

*Published by* Tughra Books
345 Clifton Ave., Clifton,
NJ, 07011, USA

www.tughrabooks.com

Library of Congress Cataloging-in-Publication Data Available

ISBN: 978-1-59784-278-5

*Printed by*
Imak Ofset, Istanbul - Turkey

# CONTENTS

## CHAPTER THREE
## AWARENESS IN EDUCATION

## CHAPTER FOUR
## RELIGIOUS EDUCATION OF THE CHILD

## CHAPTER FIVE

## DIMENSIONS OF EDUCATION

## CHAPTER SIX

## A COMPARISON BETWEEN QUR'ANIC AND NON-QUR'ANIC EDUCATION

# INTRODUCTION

## 1. Our Understanding of Morality

On certain issues, I think it's best to have a consensus before-hand with the readers. Unless we agree on the essential matters of our subject, it will not be easy to benefit from this book. It should be taken into account that it is not possible to reach a consensus with those who are not disturbed by the moral corruption of immense scale in our surroundings. First of all, for readers to benefit from this book, they need to feel pain in their hearts for the moral corruption surrounding themselves, their family, friends, and neighbors.

Throughout history, no society was lasting with immorality. I cannot tell you if any exceptions existed or not, but there is no doubt that the people who stood for a long time without being pushed aside by history were respected for their moral values.

## 2. Reasons for the Collapse of Nations

Considering past civilizations, almost all of their collapse can be attributed to a moral decay. As immorality silently undermines and gnaws the values of society, often it is not felt or realized. And when it is indeed felt, it becomes too late, similar to growing cancer going unnoticed until it causes metastasis with our sensitive points—to such a degree that late recognition of it mostly leads to death. Immorality in the life of a nation is what cancer is to the body. If those who govern the state, the heads of families, educators and the entire nation are heedless of such moral disintegration, even the noises of a national apocalypse might not stimulate them. Who knows, maybe some will take it as natural as if they were creatures that inhabit in wreckages.

When we look at history, the reasons underlying behind collapses of nations are as follows: young people's bohemian inclinations and their desire to indulge in carnal pleasures, society taking the world as the real aim and being oblivious to the Hereafter, and people turning their backs on Divine commands—erasing the awe of God from hearts and reducing everything to the material level. Almost all of these reasons exist in the collapse of so many states including the Ottomans. The depressions caused by spiritual voids were sought to be cured with worldly indulgences to worsen them completely, which meant entering a vicious cycle. However, the real problem was nation's losing their spirituality, distancing themselves from the essentials of religion, and their forgetting God. A cure was there from the real source and provider of cures for those who sought a healing for their deep wounds. However, as the material world composes one side of human reality, other worldly spirituality composes the other side. We can even say that the latter represents the human essence. The point of divergence was clear: Everything was caused by indulging in the material and neglecting the spiritual. Such a flaw could not be covered up with anything material. In fact, when the two aspects are taken in a balanced way in accordance with their measures, that is, when our duty toward God is fulfilled as becomes His greatness and when the divine revelation is respected in the same degree—in other words, when this world and the next are given their due values—then everything would be balanced. This is what the Qur'an suggests: *"Seek, by means of what God has granted you, the abode of the Hereafter, without forgetting your share in this world"* (Al-Qasas 28:77). So the blessings of God such as health, wealth, and intellect need to be utilized wisely for the afterlife, but one's decent share of the world should not be neglected; this is the measure of the Qur'an. If the balance between this world and the next was regulated according to this principle, Muslims would not be in such a wretched condition today. In our time when worldly reasons make individuals oblivious to their Creator, we wish to clarify the moral principles to be taken as basis.

Every nation has a rise and fall, with their relevant reasons. The laws operating in the universe base on a conditional causality. God Almighty created nature as superficially dependent on the rules of causality. Therefore, we are supposed to comply with these laws prevalent in the universe. If we neglect our duties by relying on their tolerance, we will be eliminated and vanished. They do not operate with any forgiveness. God Almighty does forgive His creatures; however, laws of creation do not have a forgiving nature at all. If we follow the correct methods and act in conformity with these laws, God elevates us to the highest level. On the other hand, if we fail to fulfill the requirement of causes—if there is no special Divine conduct—we might fall to the lowest of the low (see At-Tin 95:5).

Going back to the problem we mentioned at the beginning, we need to find answers to the following questions: Are there serious factors and some objective reasons for the corruption of morality? Are there really such things as a moral depression? Do the haphazard lifestyles prevalent in our time lack morality, or are they to be accepted as normal?

## 3. Imitating Other Nations

The Messenger of God, peace and blessings be upon him, warned his community about the situation of the nations that collapsed due to moral disintegration, and foretold that they would follow the way of the previous ones step by step.[1]

The societies which collapse through moral corruption experience some failures beforehand: falling for this world, and failing to set the balance between body and soul. Unfortunately, this failure, which dates back deep into history, has continued though generations in different ages. In the end, the West inherited it, and after decorating it with the fantasies of its own civilization, they passed it on to their imitators. From this perspective, the above mentioned *hadith* can be considered as a miraculous statement since it foretold a fact proven by history. It was a Divine inspiration to the Messenger of God, who expressed the meaning in words.

Here, I would like to underline another point. Material welfare of people of certain countries can make us think in the first sight that they have overcome all problems and have attained happiness. As a matter of fact, modern societies are restless deep inside in a quest for happiness, which they fail to find. Suicide rate is considerably high in the "developed" countries in comparison to other countries. A society whose individuals commit suicide in such a high rate cannot be considered happy.

---

[1]  *Sahih al-Bukhari*, "Anbiya" 50; "I'tisam" 14; *Sahih Muslim*, "Ilm" 6.

## 4. The Honorable Creature

Everything should be oriented toward the true happiness of humanity. Human beings are the vicegerent of God on earth and the focus of Divine Names. God has ordered the universe according to human beings. In this respect, civilizations must exist for humans and every civilization must target the happiness of humans. Above all, human beings are the most honorable creatures. The Qur'an decrees:

> We have honored the children of Adam (with many distinctions): We have sustained their traveling on the land and the sea, and provided for them (their sustenance) out of pure, wholesome things, and preferred them with particular preferment above many of those whom We have created. (Al-Isra 17:70).

A human being is honorable in the sight of God. All of the civilizations in history and all of the political, economical, and cultural systems acknowledge the value of the human with their very existence. Therefore, the systems established without targeting human happiness have no value and they promise nothing in the name of humanity.

## 5. The Authority of the Church and Clergy in the West

There is an important difference between the Islamic and Western worlds. In the West, the rise of science broke the authority of the Church. In the Islamic world, contrary to the West, progress in science caused more people to turn towards religion. Before the Renaissance and Reformation, individuals in Europe paid heavy taxes to the Church and the future seemed gloomy to them. Religious leaders had a negative stance against science and new inventions were rejected without being shown any tolerance. The number of people condemned by the Inquisition was high. People could not speak up against oppression. With the exception of a limited number of Aristocrats, everybody—particularly the poor—suffered greatly. Anything such as "women's rights" was out of question. In different workplaces, a woman was regarded as a half-person and received a half of the normal payment. Consequently, almost every class had become bitter against religion. Owing to this general dislike, everything that belonged to the Church came down. As the Church collapsed with this violent quake, moral values were demolished as well.

## 6. The Relation Between State and Religion in Islam

In the Islamic world, no scientist was discouraged. Religion never had pressure on the state or people at all. Might was always under the command of right, and the rulers were in the service of the people. In the face of a righteous word spoken in the name of truth, even rulers could bow down, showing their readiness to accept what was right. The well known story between Mehmed the Conqueror and the judge Khidr Chalabi is an example of this.[2]

The Rightly Guided Caliphs such as Umar ibn al-Khattab or Ali ibn Abi Talib, were brought to court in an equal status with a Jewish man. Since might sided with the right, a level of oppression to the degree that was seen in the West was never experienced in the Islamic world. Therefore, nobody was bitter against religion. The life others sought in utopias was a reality in this world.

## 7. Moral Principles

So what is right and what is wrong for us? How would we like our children to be brought up? Is there a particular project we plan in our mind? What are the values that we wish for our child to learn? What do we do in practice to have them acquire those values? For example, do we care about their hanging around outside until late at night? Are we to open our door as if nothing happened no matter how late they come? What is our measure of morality, and what is considered moral or immoral for us?

How far will we allow our children to go? Are we to have a principle for stating our opinion about their clothes?

If we are not pleased with what has happened so far, what have we planned till now? Is there a solution we have tried? Have we sought solutions that were seriously enough, such as visiting specialists and shedding tears with this concern? These questions can be directed at our-

---

2   The sultan was infuriated with a mistake made by a Christian architect and ordered him to be punished. The man sued the sultan and—to his surprise—the judge decreed that the sultan had committed injustice and deserved to be punished. On hearing the decree, the sultan drew his sword and said that he would behead the judge if he had ruled unjustly and favored the sultan. In response to this, the judge produced the mace he had been hiding and replied that he would have hit the sultan's head if he had asked to be favored.

selves, a relative, a neighbor, or people in general. So have we sought a solution in the true sense?

If we have no plans regarding these issues, then it means that we are following the footsteps of those who came before us and falling into the same pitfalls, as expressed by the Noble Messenger of God. In actual fact, the underlying reason for all of these is pushing aside God, His Noble Messenger, peace and blessings be upon him, and the principles of the Qur'an and worshipping our whims and desire instead.

Today, almost all of us have a child of our own about whom we more or less complain about. What would we think as we see their inconsistent behaviors? It is very significant even simply being able to think about it. We need to think about it! We should ponder over the question, "Indeed, what can we do in regards to this issue?" I wonder if we are tolerant or harsh or indifferent. Do we just watch the happenings in our houses emotionlessly or do we seek a solution each day?

It is possible to add more such questions. For instance, do we make an effort, like a trustee does, to follow and to get to know our child's friends? Do we prepare a healthy environment for our child? What kind of friends have we introduced to our child so far? Is it enough to register our child to a school or to personally hand them to a teacher? Even further, is it enough to just show them where the mosque is or instead to introduce them to the imam?

In addition to finding answers to these intermingled questions, the order, depth, sincerity, resolution, and its specific allure is also very important.

## 8. Living Principle-centered

It is very important to determine our lives as a "corpus of principles" from the very beginning. We should be able to say, "My years to come are planned as follows..." If we say this, then we will be faced with the known facts that we have already designed and planned, we will be able to make decisions easily, and will never get confused. However, if we do not have any decision or principle for the sake of the future, we may be drifted to unknown risks, feeling perplexed. Just imagine how these flock of unknown threats are coming to us once, we would probably moan with regret and sorrow. Thus, we should absolutely have made a decision beforehand.

Now, let's have a look at the Muslims in the world, with a population of 1.5 billion. In the oven where parents are in the fire, the flames of which rise to the sky, the children and grandchildren are also in the fire. We see that one is getting burned while the other is extremely in indifference. While a nation or several nations are sinking in the same swamp, those masses coming afterwards are also sinking in the same place, by walking inattentively, and they become like charmless souvenirs.

The Messenger of God warns us in this issue expressing that people would follow the way of the previous ones step by step.[3]

It is possible to interpret his warning as follows: "Be careful! Walk as if you are in a mine field. Always be ready for a probable explosion in any time."

In this context, Turkish poet Mehmet Akif depicts the position of a Muslim as follows:

*Modesty has been raised, shamelessness all around,*
*What ugly faces that thin veil proves to have disguised!*
*No fidelity, no loyalty to promise, not a sign of the word "trust,"*
*Lies are favored, betrayal required, right is out of sight.*
*Merciless hearts, low emotions; consuming desires*
*The meaning that flows over from the gazes is full of contempt for the servants of God.*
*How dreadful, my Lord, how shocking revolution it is*
*No religion, no faith left; religion destroyed; faith razed to the ground*
*Let virtues be ignored, let consciences fall into silence.*
*If this moral corruption lasts, there will remain no independence.*[4]

The morality of chaos and devastation can be seen not only in one place, but everywhere. So much so, that even those who are restless about this are simply unaware of all the happenings as if they are senseless.

## 9. High Morality

God's Messenger once said: "I was sent to complete and perfect high morals."[5] God has given limitless bounties to us, and we have capacities

3  *Sahih al-Bukhari*, "Anbiya" 50; "I'tisam" 14; *Sahih Muslim*, "Ilm" 6.
4  Ersoy, Mehmet Akif, *Safahat*, (vol. 7, pp. 443–444), edited by Ertuğrul Düzdağ, İstanbul: Çağrı Yayınları, 2008.
5  Ibn Abdilberr, *At-Tamhid* 16/254; Al-Bayhaki, *As-Sunanu'l-Kubra* 10/191.

to be developed. We, as human beings, are equipped with faculties and capabilities that give us the potential to have our place among the inhabitants of the Highest Rank (*Mala al-A'la*). To appreciate these blessings from God is a prerequisite, not only for due reverence toward Him, but also for respect towards ourselves who are endowed with so many potentialities. Divine books are the voices of this message and Prophets are the most steadfast agents of this truth while the final ring of this golden chain is the most lustrous proof of this truth and the most exceptional sultan of the sublime morality.

The Holy Qur'an points out the praiseworthy qualities of God's Messenger in the verse: *"You are surely of a sublime character, and do act by a sublime pattern of conduct."* (Al-Qalam 68:4) and also in the verse *"This (what we do) is the pattern of conduct of (all our) predecessors."* (Ash-Shu'ara 26:137).

## 10. The Decorations of Worldly Life

The Holy Qur'an points out the position of wealth and children in this life with the following verse:

> Wealth and children are an adornment of the present, worldly life, but the good, righteous deeds (based on faith and) which endure are better in the sight of your Lord in bringing reward and better to aspire for. (Al-Kahf 18:46).

These adornments are on the transient face of the world, which fades, withers, deteriorates, and irritates. Therefore the gains of this life are not a source of pride. Even one's sons and daughters are not a source of pride. However, if these adornments are turned to God, they become priceless and attain the level of "the good, righteous deeds (based on faith) which endure." When they become the good and righteous deeds, they appear like a huge fruitful tree in the Hereafter, while they are just mere seeds in this life.

The Holy Qur'an provides us the principles which determine the most suitable method to handle these significant issues. The remedies can be found in the "mighty pharmacy" of the Qur'an, and in the system established by the auspicious and blessed hands of the Messenger of God.

As for paying attention to the sublime call of the revelation and *sunnah,* it is entirely a matter of seeking a share from the Divine bounties.

## 11. To Be Merciful

The Holy Qur'an points out that people facing various problems should take refuge in the compassion of God, as stated in the example of Prophet Job.[6] Taking refuge in His mercy and compassion means demanding for the Divine aid from His Mercy for our own souls, families, children, and relatives. This also means declaring our own weakness and frailty, and accepting and confessing His Omnipotence. In addition, mercy is a means of mercy. If someone is merciful, God is also merciful to him or her. If we are sensitive against degeneration and decay, then He protects us against such kind of risks.

The Messenger of God, peace and blessings be upon him, declares as follows:

> Show mercy and clemency toward the creatures on earth (particularly those innocent children) so that the dwellers of heavens (and God) show mercy to you.[7]

True death and calamity is not one that is caused by ordinary accidents. True death and calamity is emerging one's essence in heedlessness, becoming senseless and dying in the world of heart. The greatest disaster is not being able to know the fire inside the house, i.e. being senseless against the decay of a child.

If parents are unaware of the spiritual fire in the house, it is the greatest unfortunateness, indolence, and misguidance. It would be very proper if such people cry for their states day and night; however crying demands a sound and healthy spiritual heart.

## 12. The Highest Rank of Humanity

Moral corruption is a tremendous disaster. Therefore, we believe that the moral principles in the Qur'an are a source of healing for those who are in depression.

---

6  See Al-Anbiya 21:83.
7  *Sunan at-Tirmidhi,* "Birr" 16; *Sunan Abu Dawud,* "Adab" 58.

The Holy Qur'an points out a fact as follows:

Surely We have created human of the best stature, as the perfect pattern of creation; Then We have reduced him to the lowest of the low. (At-Tin 95:4–5).

It is possible to interpret this verse as follows: "We have created human being in the best form and nature, and then pushed him to the lowest of the low." In other words, "We put them in a state where they should always struggle with their evil-commanding souls, where they sometimes fall down, but they can also soar to the highest rank of humanity with the wings of faith and good deeds."

This verse of the Holy Qur'an takes us under its wing, holds our hands, and takes us to the highest rank of humanity; it takes us from moral corruption, the lowest of the low, helplessness, and clumsiness to the highest of the high. We will try to present the luminous messages of the Qur'an on these issues in the following chapters.

# Chapter One

## MARRIAGE

# MARRIAGE

## 1. Education of the Family

"What do you think about the general course of events in the world? What do you feel about unacceptable, amoral behavior that is all around? What is your reaction to them? What is the solution to such problems?"

If we are not happy with the current situation of the world, if we feel ill at ease in our hearts, and if we are dissatisfied with those who have caused the problems, what solution can be offered? Undoubtedly, these are issues with which we must become familiar.

Believers take all prayers seriously, and for them avoiding these prayers because of their discipline is obviously not a very favorable attitude. At the same time, wandering the streets aimlessly, or causing trouble as a pastime are frowned upon by believers, although some consider these activities as fundamental parts of freedom. In this chapter, what is ethical and what is unethical in Islam will be examined, and education in the light of the Qur'an and within the framework of its principles will be discussed.

The most important basis of ethics is faith and the principles of belief. However, not everything is comprised of these principles only. If people do not practice their belief in everyday life, in other words, if they do not complement their belief with activities of worship, or if they do not behave in a way that is in accord with their belief system, then belief remains no more than thought. Such a life does not influence or shape the personal lives of individuals or that of their familial or social lives. In fact, faith is a light and a source of strength while lack of faith is futility and weakness. Real faith takes its strength from practice. A person without faith can never be of use to society; useful people are so rare that their number does not exceed the number of the fingers on one hand. For example, a person may not be a believer, yet, at the same time, he or she may be virtuous. I am not sure whether such people can be considered as virtuous from the perspective of the fundamental principles, as the real virtue is the virtue that is derived from faith (by seeking the pleasure of God only, not derived from personal egotistic desires) and the questioning of one's activities. Indeed, belief in God, the Hereafter, the holy books, the resurrection, and Heaven and Hell are the important principles that elevate our lives to the level of the angels and that bring order to our lives.

It is imperative that these issues be practiced in everyday life. The Hereafter is a courtroom in which our existence in this world will be thoroughly examined; in fact, it is a place where we will be questioned as to whether we have been sufficiently thankful to God who has created us as human beings in a perfect manner in this world. There are also an infinite number of tyrants and ungrateful people who insist on not seeing the obvious art of God and ignore all those beauties by closing their eyes; deaf people who insist on not hearing thousands of melodies; and heartless people who are unfaithful and ungrateful and who do not appreciate the harmony of the colors, the sounds, the patterns, the nuances, and the order of the universe. God will establish His court so that the believers will be distinguished from such people in the Hereafter. He will also prepare the Heaven and the Hell; those who have lived a virtuous life in this world and whose hearts were open to lofty feelings will be entitled to the heavens, which they have been promised. Virtuous people have reached the level of "perfect human" in this world.

Indeed, a believer is an individual who considers all of these things and orders his or her life accordingly. For this reason, the most important thing is that belief should be very strong, both in the individual and in society, so that believers can seek protection in it against various emotions that may lead them astray. The families or societies made up of members of weak faith are not sound families or societies. Such societies cannot form good nations. Individuals must have a strong faith in the Hereafter so that they can become closer to God and become useful members of their society.

Indeed, it is essential that everyone has such a strong faith that without practice of his or her belief in this world they would be questioned in the presence of God. Individuals who have such faith and with the centrifugal force of such a conviction will incline to performing good deeds, and will prostrate themselves, laying their faces on the floor, so that they will be able to appear in the presence of God with honor.

Families that consist of such members will be dealt with in another chapter. We will also deal with some aspects of the family, and how the younger generation, in particular small children, should be educated concerning Islamic ethical principles in the light of verses from the Qur'an and the traditions (*Hadith*s) of the Prophet, peace and blessings be upon him, in the following chapters.

Children and wealth are the embellishments and ornaments of this world.[8] If one deals with these gifts in a proper manner, they will also be abundant benefactors in the Hereafter. God rejoices with such servants and fills people's hearts with happiness. He makes such people ornaments to the eye and food for the heart. Whenever you see one of these people, you are made aware of the happiness of this world in your actions as well as the pleasure of the next world in your hopes. However, if you cannot make these ornaments last forever, you will never be truly happy; even if you are happy, there will always be something missing in your life. Indeed, your children, your grandchildren, and your world will all make you uneasy. If you change these temporal ornaments which are doomed to vanish to become everlasting, and if you look after them in the Name of God Almighty, and use and improve them in the path that He wants and the direction that He asks you to follow, you would realize that every point which is seen as the final stop in fact is a starting point; all temporary ornaments, magnificence, and glorious possessions will become perfected and will continue to exist in the next world.

## 2. The Importance of the Home

The attainment of a perfect society starts from the home, that is, from families that are built together by husband and wife. Any lasting education starts from the family. An enlightened society is unattainable if the family is not founded on principles of education. Moreover, even though a thorough educational program is very important for the development of the younger generation in any society, it is always the home that remains as the essential building block; the family has much to offer society.

---

[8]   See Al-Kahf 18:46.

Minds that can be nurtured within the family, especially during the subconscious period of development, might later surprise us by utilizing these subconscious accumulations to become great people in the future; of course there is always the need for some minor reminders to keep these young heroes sheltered from ill winds. Indeed, a successful home-life is the first step towards general success in life. Ultimately, this first step depends on a healthy marriage.

## 3. The Purpose of Marriage

The family is not, as some authors have claimed, a factory for the pro-duction of children. It is the most essential part of society and the first seed of the nation. Thus, it is neither a means of maintaining the birth rate nor one of sexual satisfaction. It is a holy institution. The most obvi-ous indicator of this holiness is the institution of marriage. Matrimony has been defined as the act of bringing couples together within certain principles and through a legitimate contract with an obvious purpose. God sees all relationships that do not occur within the principles of mat-rimony as being adulterous.

Religion considers this legitimate union as the foundation and basis of the nation. Since purposeless, random, or aimless marriages challenge legitimate guidelines, a Muslim must exercise caution concerning his or her marriage. The purpose of marriage should be to raise future genera-tions that will attain the consent of God and the pleasure of His Messen-ger, peace and blessings be upon him.

Marriages that are not built upon a purpose are graceless, in the same way that good deeds become barren if they are performed without intention. Relationships that appear to be a matrimonial union, if made merely on the basis of physical considerations, have no other-wordly concerns and later become causes for bitter disputes between spouses. In cases of confessional discord where someone who believes in the Qur'an and recognizes God's Messenger marries a person who refuses to believe, i.e. if there are opposing beliefs in terms of faith, religious and doctrinal disputes become unavoidable.

The "purposeful marriage" is one that has been carefully calculated and which is not only emotional but also rational. If purpose is the moti-vation behind a marriage, then there will be peace in the family. Marriages that are made without thinking about the consequences and purposes will end in problems.

Religion, which, on the one hand, not only makes marriage legitimate and acts as a great incentive towards it, puts forth the condition of "purpose" on the other. All individuals must already have a purpose in all of their actions and must work so that they are determined in their efforts, consequently enabling them to reach their goal. With no purpose in life, no one can organize his or her time and they cannot achieve anything in this life, nor in the Hereafter. Having a purpose in everything is a method and a system. It is a fact that, if we do not take into consideration intention in our actions and behavior, then we are destined to greatly miss out on many opportunities.

## 4. The Conditions of Marriage

The importance religion places on marriage is beyond any estimation. Likewise, the *fuqaha* (the religious experts on the everyday life of the Muslims) also take the issue of matrimony very seriously, and as a consequence have written volumes of books on the matter. The issue of marriage has been arranged into categories, such as *fard* (obligatory, the religious duty of all Muslims), *wajib* (essential, mandatory, incumbent on a Muslim), *sunnah* (a practice performed or advised by the Prophet, but not obligatory), *haram* (forbidden by religion, unlawful, illicit), and *makruh* (disliked or discouraged); all of these are connected with the circumstances of the individual. No one can marry arbitrarily; some people should marry when they are under certain circumstances, while others should not, for various reasons.

Thus, if a person gets married without taking into consideration all the aspects of these issues, but rather just jumps into marriage merely in order to satisfy sexual desires, it is extremely doubtful that such a person will establish a healthy family or bring up children that will be a useful and well-adjusted members of society.

The arguments of the scholars of the Hanafi and Maliki schools do not greatly differ from one another on this issue. The disagreements between them are in the details. If we are to arrange the issues of matrimony according to these great scholars, then we can classify them as follows:[9]

## a) The Obligatory (*Fard*) Marriage

If someone feels uncomfortable with unbearable sexual drive and is afraid that he might not show resistance to the danger of committing adultery or other related sins or, according to some scholars, if such a person cannot fast (to restrain his carnal desires), then that person must marry as soon as he can financially support a family and when he is able to pay the *mahr*, the obligatory dowry given to the bride for her use only in order to honor her and as a proof of groom's willingness to marry her.

In other words, marriage is essential to prevent a person from falling into illicit activities, and when a person is confronted by such *haram* situations, the only choice to be made here is marriage. Avoiding marriage through unusual or unnatural means is no different from fighting one's very nature. Any person who attempts such a battle is doomed to failure.

## b) The Essential or Mandatory (*Wajib*) Marriage

If someone is able to pay a dowry and support a family and is not in any "real" danger of committing a sin, yet there is a concern that a sin might be committed, then it is essential for that individual to marry. This is not a commonly held view; it is supported by only a minority of scholars.

## c) The Sunnah Marriage

A *sunnah* marriage is one where there is no apparent danger and a person willingly desires to get married.

## d) The Forbidden (*Haram*) Marriage

If by way of marriage one is going to fall into the sin of earning money unlawfully, such as taking bribes, stealing, or becoming involved in deceit, in order to support his family, then marriage for this person is forbidden, or at the very least is undesirable. Some scholars are also of the view that if a person is thought to be psychologically unfit for mar-

---

[9]  See, Wahba Suhayli, *İslam Fıkıh Ansiklopedisi*, 9/28–31.

riage, i.e. if he may bring harm to his wife or future children, then such a person should not marry at all.

### e) The Undesirable (*Makruh*) Marriage

According to some scholars, if there is some worry that a person might commit sins or might bring harm to his wife when he marries, then such a marriage becomes undesirable.

### f) The Permissible (*Mubah*) Marriage

If a person earns his living lawfully, is not in danger of falling into adultery, and is capable of paying the dowry and supporting his family, then the marriage of such a person is acceptable and desirable. Such a person may marry if he wishes or he may remain celibate.

Imam Shafi remarks that matrimony is intrinsically an ordinary action, in other words, it is a permissible action. Yet, in the case of avoiding sins, it becomes essential or obligatory. In fact, the views of the Shafi School on marriage are similar to that of the Hanafi School. Imam Ahmad ibn Hanbal believes that whether or not a person is able to support himself and his family, whether or not he can pay the dowry, whether or not he is in apparent danger of falling into sin, such as adultery, it is incumbent on everybody to marry. In fact, these disagreements are not great if one examines the matter carefully and in detail.

Here it has been shown that in religion, concerning matrimony, purposes and intentions are involved, and that marriage is not simply a normal everyday action that is to be taken lightly. If this important decision of one's life is not based on sound, logical reasoning, then eventually the courtrooms will become frequented by lonely spouses and parentless children. Religion tries to forestall these problems; it classifies certain marriages as forbidden or undesirable from the very start. Reason and logic in what is essentially an emotional union are emphasized.

Matrimony is a very serious decision, as it is the true foundation of the family, the most important element of society. For this reason, when matrimony is considered, it should be taken seriously, not abandoning the decision to the sensual or sexual desires of the individual. In other words, marriage should be treated as a religious, national, and universal issue that is closely related to the complete happiness of the society as a whole. As to the material and biological needs of the individual, marriage is a gift granted by God in advance in return for this service to maintain human race and to raise new generations with excellent qualities will be nurtured, making our future a success.

Islam places a great emphasis on this issue. One should consider every single aspect of marriage, thinking about all the possibilities and behaving in order to avoid all wrongful actions. Thus, homes will not be founded on misguided principles that may lead to their eventual destruction.

### g) Evidence from the Qur'an and the hadith

1. The Messenger of God recommends marriage: "Marry and multiply so that I will be proud of your numerousness."[10]
2. In another *hadith* he again recommends that the Muslim men prefer to marry women who are also willing to raise a family and would agree to have children.[11]
3. In a verse from the Holy Qur'an God says:

Marry those among you who are single (whether men or women) and those of your male and female slaves that are righteous (and fit for marriage). If they are poor, God will grant them sufficiency out of His bounty. God is All-Embracing in His mercy, All-Knowing. (An-Nur 24:32)[12]

As to those who do not have sufficient financial resources to get married, in other words, those who cannot give alms or pay the dowry, or those who simply cannot support a family, such people should endure and continue to live an honorable life without falling into forbidden actions until God makes them rich with His grace.

Therefore, the *hadith* stating "Marry and multiply so that I will be proud of your numerousness" reminds us, explicitly and implicitly, that if the marriage should not aim to make the Prophet proud, then such a union or multiplication is deemed as naught. It is obvious that the

---

[10] Abd al-Razzak, *Musannaf*, 6/173; Ajluni, *Kashf al-Hafa*, 1/318–319.
[11] *Sunan Abu Dawud*, "Nikah" 3; *Sunan an-Nasa'i*, "Nikah" 11.
[12] This is not a compulsory order; as marriage depends on the choice of an individual. However, if a person wants to marry, but cannot afford it, those responsible for them among their relatives or, in case of their being without relatives, the state, should arrange their marriage.

Prophet would not be pleased with a generation that is indulged in terrorism and corruption, a generation that has left prayer, and that act as cold-blooded murderers. The generation that he wants to multiply is a generation that lives and helps to endure the true and accepted religion he brought. The Holy Qur'an is the best reference point with its crystal clear statements:

> Wealth and children are an adornment of the present, worldly life, but the good, righteous deeds (based on faith and) which endure are better in the sight of your Lord in bringing reward and better to aspire for. (Al-Kahf 18:46).

Indeed, if you live keeping the Hereafter in mind, it can be said that you have entered on the path of pleasing your Lord and in return, He will be pleased with you.

The conclusion that we can arrive at after considering these evidence is that the essential purpose of marriage is to raise a generation that is both pleasing to God and His Prophet. For this reason, individuals who are pious, who are responsible citizens, who will be fond of their families and interested in the education of their children should never have doubts about parenting children in a legitimate way, as an increase in the population of such a generation would definitely be a means of pleasure for the Prophet.

In the light of the preceding arguments, the recommendation of the Messenger of God to the young people is of great importance: "O the community of youth! Those who have the means to marry should marry. Those who cannot marry should fast, as this is a shield against the forbidden acts."[13]

Fasting has the function of diet. It helps person to take their hunger and other feelings under strict control in such a way that he or she may perform the religious duties in accordance with the commands of God. It is hoped that a person who cannot marry can protect himself from committing sin by way of holding the reins of carnal desires by fasting until they can have the financial means for marriage.

---

[13] *Sahih al-Bukhari*, "Nikah" 2; *Sahih Muslim*, "Nikah" 1/3; "Siyam" 43; *Sunan ibn Majah*, "Nikah" 1.

Marriage is such a serious issue that one cannot make a decision concerning it without careful consideration, while at the same time it is such a deceptively simple action that one would find it difficult to realize its importance without thinking seriously about its possible consequences. An arbitrary decision about marriage, without paying attention to the logical and rational aspects involved, will eventually lead to disputes and conflicts in family life. Children raised in such conflicting surrounding will grow up insensible and hostile to their community, perhaps even towards their own parents.

This is exactly the situation that we are witnessing today in many societies around the globe. Indeed, in many countries marriage is not taken seriously and it is not based on certain principles. This essential and vital institution is perceived as being no more than a means of satisfying the material needs of human beings, much as one seeks to satisfy one's hunger with food. The framework of its intention is narrowed and becomes meaningless. No nation made up of degenerate individuals will be able to remain on the surface of the earth for a long time.

## 5. The Principles of Primordial Nature in Marriage

### a) The Beginning of Every Good Deed: In the Name of God

Couples who have succeeded in establishing a home based on the above principles have achieved something truly important. Such homes, while performing their roles as "Houses of God" operate as temples or schools, enabling the winds of revival to waft through the whole nation. Homes that follow the principles established by God serve society in much the same way that DNA serves the body.

There is another subject that we should give our attention to here. Before we eat, we say *"Bismillahirrahmanirrahim"* (In the Name of God, the All-Merciful and the All-Compassionate). It is believed that we gain blessings from God if we say this from the bottom of our heart.

Likewise, we seek refuge from the temptations of Satan and ask God for protection against him. In all our actions, including even the most intimate ones, we are careful about such behavior and manners. We hope that our children, for whom we plead God for help and refuge from evil, will be kind and good-tempered and that Satan will not meddle with them.

One who neglects to seek shelter in God encounter problems, often having no idea as to the reasons or sources of these problems, yet being crushed under their weight. Such matters do not tolerate failure in the fulfillment of all the requirements, the major ones as well as the minor ones. One must comply with all the conditions of this test; a test that every human being is subjected to in this world. One must never lapse into ignorance while carrying out their responsibilities; one must treat one's duties with the utmost care.

A single moment of negligence can cause severe damage, just as a momentary lapse of attention on the part of the driver at the wheel can cause great havoc. Indeed, believers should have faith and confidence and seek refuge in God. Every action should be performed with this in mind, even in matters that seem to be quite straightforward, such as matrimony. Matrimony should be carried out in the Name of God; a marriage that is not performed with a reliance on God will have no positive results. Yes, matrimony is a spiritual bond and its blessings lie in having a good relationship with God.

For this reason, matrimony must be carried out in the Name of God in order that it will be sanctified by Him. It must contain a prayer and be carried out within the principles set out by Him. God sanctifies and accepts any matrimony made in His name. Such marriages are under His protection. Marriages carried out in this way promise a shared future and bring spouses closer to one another.

In recent years the divorce rate has increased and many marriages are no longer in the realm of the grace of Divine Providence. Arbitrary and aimless marriages are entered into only in order to satisfy sexual desires; such behavior has substantially destroyed the foundations of the family institution.

## b) Selection of a Partner

The first issue that one should consider when contemplating marriage is to find a partner who is compatible with one's feelings and ideas. Many young persons these days make this life-time decision based solely on their emotions, attempting to establish a home with someone who they have met casually. Marriages that ignore or disregard its suitability, and factors like the logic of marriage and establishing a home are obviously susceptible to future problems. Candidates who want to embark on such marriages would do better to seek the advice of others, people who are perhaps not only more experienced in such matters, but who also can consider the matter from a broader perspective.

Sometimes, a marriage that is based solely on physical attraction might turn a home that is supposed to be a part of Heaven into a pit of Hell. We know many people who are recognized for their piety and religious fervor, yet who experience constant strife within the family, simply because they did not thoroughly think through their choice of partner beforehand.

In such a family, disputes are never ending. One of them may want to perform his religious duties and the other may feel uneasy. Therefore, in such a family the man and the wife are never united, they can never share the home in peace; on the contrary, they have separate lives. In such a family, two different types of books are read, two different newspapers come into the house, two different stories are told, and two separate gatherings take place. When the wife asks for something the husband refuses. The wife talks about religion, faith, and morality; the husband uses these as an excuse for an argument. In this way, two lives are being lived in one family... Can we call such a situation living?

Under such an atmosphere of tension and recrimination, children may be inclined to choose sides, or, another, more frequent, outcome, is that they will grow up torn between the two sides, causing the children to become insensitive, and finally turning them into enemies of both society and the institution of the family. Thus, when a man and a woman take steps towards marriage they must think this decision over thoroughly. They should ask for the advice of those who are experienced in these matters and ensure that their priorities are well defined. The Messenger of God gives the following advice concerning the subject: "There are four reasons why a woman is chosen for marriage: for her wealth, for her good family name, for her beauty, or for her piety. You must choose the pious one in order to attain peace."[14]

Religion is the most important factor in selecting a spouse. When choosing between two candidates, if one is beautiful and the other only of average appearance, it is the beauty of piety, morality, and religion that

---

[14] *Sahih al-Bukhari*, "Nikah" 15; *Sunan Abu Dawud*, "Nikah" 2; *Sunan an-Nasa'i*, "Nikah" 13; *Sunan ibn Maja*, "Nikah" 6.

should be chosen. Indeed, family life is not a life pertaining only to this world; it will exist over a prolonged period of time, stretching well into the next world and beyond, through our children and grandchildren. In fact, a good home can be a heavenly place on earth, yet at the same time a home can be destroyed by mistakes. The result of such errors is that the home becomes a graveyard, eventually blocking the roads to Heaven.

For this reason one must examine any future spouse's religious beliefs, actions, and especially his/her faith. Someone who agrees to marry his daughter to a person who is not concerned with religion or faith will be held responsible for all future problems. The same situation is true for a man as well. A person who does not believe in God, who takes their religious obligations lightly, has a serious "faith" problem. Therefore, the fundamental element of religion is absent in the marriage.

A marriage realized solely on material considerations, such as financial well-being, career, fame, or high salary, obviously downplays religion and faith. Those who get married under such circumstances are clearly losers in a race that they might have won. In marriage, priority should be given to religion. The foundation of religion is faith. Marriage to a faithless person cannot be considered a real marriage; it is nothing more than bringing two people together.

The arguments that we have been discussing so far apply to people who accept the laws and criteria of religion. Once again it should be emphasized that marriage is one of the most essential sources of happiness in this and in the other world. Those who make a mistake in such a serious matter extinguish the light of both of these worlds.

### c) Raising Children

Parents should always be in agreement on the matters that are involved in the raising of well-behaved, good children. Children raised by parents who possess neither the capability nor the desire to raise a child, or those who raised by parents who have capability, but lack a sense of responsibility for the problems of the child, should be considered as little more than orphans.

The mother, who is psychologically more capable at raising children, thanks to compassion and patience bestowed to her by God's mercy, should use these characteristics to raise her children to be good and useful members of society. The mother is already by nature a teacher, a trainer, and a mentor. One of the most important tasks for her should be raising her children. The tradition of the Prophet clearly indicates this exceptional role of the mother in educating children: "God will separate those persons on the Day of Judgment from their loved ones if they have separated a mother from her child in this world."[15]

While the mother is discharging her duties in accordance with her biological and psychological makeup, the father always needs to be deliberate, thoughtful, wise, and careful; these again are in compliance with his nature and standing in society. He is busy with politics, the office, commerce, agriculture, etc., and he fulfils to some degree, by his nature, a different function in the family. Indeed, he is more inclined to different tasks, because of his endurance, strength, and inherent physical differences. Since ancient times, chores that need physical work like woodcutting in the forests, plowing, growing corn and rye, heavy construction work, or laboring in factories have been expected from the father.

Furthermore, despite the fact that a man is a monument of endurance yet, he is not the epitome of compassion. Compassion is the most important characteristic in a mother; she carries her baby in her womb for nine months and ten days. She brings the baby into this world with great pain and then raises it with great effort. If the baby cries in the middle of the night she immediately runs to comfort it, taking it to her breast. She lives so that her baby will live; this is by her nature.

Today in many parts of the world, both husband and wife are working and the children are entrusted to the care of a nanny or a baby-sitter, or in many instances, at a day-care center. Indeed, if both parents are working outside the home, the children are to some extent abandoned, and they feel great loneliness. The parents console themselves by saying: "The people looking after them are caring and knowledgeable. They take care of our child much better than we could." The child, however, needs much more than this.

At a day-care centre, the child will be kept clean, his or her clothes will be looked after, his or her meals will be prepared; when the child needs a break, the day-care workers might take him or her out, for example to a park, or somewhere else. Yet these people in charge of the child can never be the same as a mother or a father. They cannot provide the

---

[15]  Hakim, *Mustadrak*, 2/55.

child with what he or she needs most. Tenderness is the most natural and innate closeness, a closeness that a child can read on the face of the mother, or find in her heart, or feel sitting snuggled up next to his or her father. Other people cannot give this tenderness to a child; they can never satisfy the child with substitutes.

Apart from the children that have been left to the care of kindergartens or day nurseries, let us now consider the situation of some children in some countries who are forced to work or sent to the care of a master so that they may learn a craft at an early age. If this master is merciless or bad tempered, these children who are treated constantly in a disheartening manner grow so mercilessly that they would not hesitate to display rudeness even towards their own parents let alone the strangers. If the negative impact that these tough and rude people might have on the delicate spirits of young children is so serious, then it would be difficult to guess the future conditions of the babies that we leave to the care of total strangers as soon as they come to this world.

God, who introduces Himself as the All-Merciful and the All-Compassionate and describes His attributes of compassion and clemency in the Qur'an exactly one hundred and fourteen times with the beautiful word *"Bismillahirrahmanirrahim"* (In the Name of God, the All-Merciful and the All-Compassionate). Indeed, we can consider the mother's great solicitude and care of her children as a manifestation of these Beautiful Names of God, with all of His great kindness and charity. There is no doubt that this cannot be exchanged with or given up for any other thing in this world.

Parents should always be on their guard and use their homes as a greenhouse, protecting their children against any possible dangers. They must prioritize the moral education of their children and should not allow them to go unnourished.

Here a final word should be said concerning the fact that parents do their best in order to raise a healthy generation, people who are attached firmly to their land, nation, and religion. They must not allow such a generation to fall into rational, emotional, and logical emptiness. If the parents are pious, upright and attached to the Qur'an and if they are practicing Muslims, their children will grow—*insha'Allah* (if God wills)—in all aspects and they will be the pride of nations.

## 6. The Great Virtues of the Mother

The mother is the most important factor in the raising of a nation. She is so sacred in the eyes of Islam that the Messenger of God reminds us that "Paradise is under the feet of the mother."[16]

This statement is true; it is the mother who acts as the sacred hand that kneads the nation and she is the founder of the home, the first step of society. She is the true founder of the home in which precious children will be the sources of great happiness.

From this perspective, Islam honors the mother with such a great esteem that to try to give her any other reward would be to degrade her; it would amount to removing a heavily ornamented crown from her head and putting in its place a cheap tiara embellished with ordinary glass. God, who has created both man and woman, has also instilled in each qualities that are suitable; these are necessarily different from one another, as each is endowed according to their capacities.

In fact, a woman has been given such qualities that she is actually far ahead of man. She is very graceful and a hero of mercy; she is so bonded to her children that the father cannot even compete with her in this respect. This situation is not unique to humanity; a hen may sacrifice her life, even though that is her only possession in this world, in order to save her chick from the bite of a dog. For this reason, the enduring compassion instilled in all creatures by God towards their offspring is a characteristic of the high status of the mother; any other position you may give her will always remain under the shadow of what God has already given her.

In this chapter which we have only touched on matters very briefly; we have tried to give our readers a general idea of how a home should be established. We have discussed faith, the practical aspects of Islam, the religiosity of the couples, the division of labor among husband and wife, and how a couple should help one another to raise children with good manners and morals. We have also emphasized some of the sensitive issues involved in becoming a community of which the Messenger of God, peace and blessings be upon him, would be proud. We intend to touch on the framework of the family in the next chapter.

---

[16] Ajluni, *Kashf al-Hafa*, 1/355; see also *Sunan an-Nasa'i*, "Jihad" 6; *Sunan ibn Majah*, "Jihad" 12.

# Chapter Two

---

## FAMILY

# FAMILY

## 1. What Kind of Family?

In the previous chapter the family or home as one of the most important units (institutions) of society and observing religious principles within a family were discussed. In order to ensure the best possible results the establishment of a family is a matter that must be taken seriously from the very beginning and an excellent plan is needed before embarking on married life. Any undertaking that is not seriously considered in the planning phase and that is not based on sound rationale may face insurmountable problems at later stages.

The family is the most important unit of any society. If this unit is strong then the nation and the state will be strong. Therefore, the family, the foundation of nations and states, should not be something that is embarked upon without previous contemplation and the drawing up of a plan; any negligence in this regard entails negligence for the entire nation. Therefore, we believe that considerable emphasis should be put upon the importance of the family. We would like to affirm our belief once more that illegitimate unions may damage the health of society.

A family established on a passing whim, momentary pleasure, or passion, or one that is entered into out of spite without any long-term purpose have no future and they remain potential sources of trouble. Such a home environment will produce negligence and the children of such will be more likely to have anti-social tendencies continuously breed street gangs because such a family has not been established according to a plan or a program that can generate blessing and fertility. We name this plan "marriage," and on the path to marriage selfishness and trivial desires should be abandoned and reason and love should become the dominant forces. We also believe that giving central importance to religious beliefs in such a marriage is very beneficial. If the husband and wife have no relationship with Almighty God, then there is little likelihood that their children will be conscious, sentient, and well-adjusted or settled; nor is it likely that they will have a fully developed sense of responsibility. To achieve positive results when establishing a family is very difficult; if a family is successful in this, then this is an exceptional blessing from Almighty God and we should be grateful to Him.

In fact, everything in this universe we live is connected to a cause. By taking into account the causes of things, with the blessing and help of Almighty God, we can quite frequently achieve the desired result in our affairs. If we disregard the cause when we try to do something, our attempts will fail to produce the desired results. Therefore, if we do not want to suffer loss and failure we should carefully consider the causes and the background of every issue with great care, and even then we can only hope for positive results from God, putting our full trust in His blessings. Our trust in Almighty God must be complete and thorough when making decisions. However, up until the point when we, with full trust, submit the matter to God, we must ensure that we have taken all the necessary steps, not neglecting any point; the actions that need to be performed are a type of physical prayer. The explanation of such behavior is found in the Islamic principle "resorting to necessary measures (*asbab*—worldly causes) is not an obstacle to being resigned (to the will of God)—*tawakkul*."

Any principles concerned with the raising of healthy generations will have meaning only after one has accepted the necessity of establishing a family in the manner described above. Nevertheless, if there are any problems in the basic makeup of a family, any attempts to solve these will lose their effect in proportion to the seriousness of the problem. In a family that has been established with blessings and sincerity, i.e. in families built upon the union of virtuous men and women, faithful men and women, people who carry out their responsibilities, everything will work well. Such a home is like a heavenly palace. I feel that the cries of children born into these types of families are as sacred as an angel's remembrance of Almighty God and they are regarded as a form of prayer.

The Qur'an focuses on both men and women when discussing a healthy and well functioning society. It describes the attitudes and behaviors of men and women in a sound society as follows:

Surely all men and women who submit to God, and all truly believing
men and women and truly believing women, and all devoutly obedient men and
devoutly obedient women, and all men and women honest and truthful in
their speech, and all men and women who persevere (in obedience to God
through all adversity), and all men and women humble (in mind and heart
before God), and all men and women who give in charity, and all men and
women who fast, and all men and women who guard their chastity, and
all men and women who remember and mention God much—for them
God has prepared forgiveness (to bring unforeseen blessings) and a tremendous reward. (Al-Ahzab 33:35)

These men and women are united as believers and Muslims in a
family, the smallest unit of society; they put their trust in God and are
sincerely committed to His existence and are within Divine companion-
ship. After being united as a family they spend their life in praying and
remembrance of Him.

The words that are uttered by men and women of faith do not contradict their behavior, nor do their acts refute what they say. In such
families, everything is in order and everything is as it appears. Children
who grow up in such a family environment will always behave properly,
seeing their parents as examples. The family environment and parental
behavior are the mirrors in which children can see themselves. When
they emulate their parents they are behaving as they should; they witness
neither behavior nor words that contradict reality. Whatever happens in
such a family is necessarily correct, due to the faithful men and women
at its center.

These women and men are patient and responsible believers in full
consciousness of observing prayer and carrying out good deeds, as well
as shouldering the burdens of any misfortunes that they may face; such
women and men, who persistently guard themselves from transgressing
and who perceive the doing of evil as being no less than passing through
the gates of Hell, will have a great influence not only on their children,
but also on their social environment. Their codes of conduct will have so
great an effect that I think their exemplary behavior will carry more
weight than their words.

The family atmosphere generated will be one where children will
possess only an abundant respect for God, with devotion, tenderness,
sobriety, and attentiveness; such will be an environment where an awe of

God is constantly felt, where the family members carry out their responsibilities to the best of their ability, being aware of the formidable fate awaiting them. In such an environment, the Hereafter is remembered at every moment. Children in such families will see a gentle anxiety on their parents' faces, an expression that encourages pleasant feelings to accompany this awe. Children will see cheerfulness and delight reflected in the faces of their loved ones, reflections of the love of God and their desire for Paradise. Children who have seen such things in their families will grow up comfortable in themselves, but conscientious; happy yet far-sighted. They will enjoy their life, yet at the same time they will grow as people with a hope for the future.

To encourage a spirit of generosity in children, the mother and father should give freely to charity and be willing to do favors for others. If we, as parents are not generous, our children will not have an example of what being generous means. I once encountered a very interesting situation: A husband and a wife were continuously giving to charity, but they hid it from one another. One did not inform the other about their donations. There is one thing that is certain here that they both were charitable persons. A child growing up in such a family would stand a good chance of becoming a benevolent person, like his/her parents.

A family composed of a husband and wife who both fast as prescribed by God (not just staying hungry for a whole day, but also restraining oneself from all kinds of evil and wrongdoing), and the society and nation based on such families are all candidates for another dimension of peace and security.

In addition to such qualities, people in devout families are very aware of and careful to respect their fidelity, honor, and purity. While they live, they live for their beliefs (religion) and their fidelity. Such people will attain happiness in this world and in the Hereafter. The family structure established in the Qur'an is based on both men and women, perceiving them together as two threads of the most sacred of all fabrics. If within the family there is a love for the nation, the children and the grandchildren will inherit the same spirit that permeates the family atmosphere. Social solidarity and salvation depend upon the transmission of this spirit to and its continuation in all members of family, that is, among all parts of society. All other systems that disregard this fact are nothing more than mere fantasy.

Now let us look at society, marriage, the family, and what makes a happy home from a different perspective.

## 2. Children

When the issue of having children is looked at in the light of Divine decree (scriptural texts—*nass*), it is obvious that there is a desire in the Qur'an for there to be more people for God to love and be pleased with. All of the Prophets, saints and other righteous people have also stated that they desire for there to be more people of a devout nature and they have developed systems to try to achieve this state.

In the Qur'an we are reminded of the Prophet Zachariah's appeal and supplication to God:

> At that point, Zachariah turned to his Lord in prayer and said: "My Lord, bestow upon me out of Your grace a good, upright offspring. Truly, You are the Hearer of prayer." (Al-Imran 3:38)

If one studies this plea one can see that Zachariah did not simply wish for "offspring," but rather emphasized an "upright offspring." Here we can see that wishing for an "upright offspring" is something that pleases God, pleases the Prophet, and makes the father happy; to wish for such means to wish for a child that will make an important contribution to the society as well. When building the Ka'ba with his son Ishmael, Abraham, may peace be upon them, appealed to God as follows:

> Our Lord! Make us Muslims, submissive to You, and of our offspring a community Muslim, submissive to You. Show us our rites of worship and accept our repentance. Surely You are the One Who accepts repentance and returns it with liberal forgiveness and additional reward, the All-Compassionate. (Al-Baqara 2:128).

The fact that the Pride of Humanity, the Prophet Muhammad, peace and blessings be upon him, and hundreds of other Prophets came from their progeny is an indication that this prayer was accepted. All the devout and faithful followers of the Prophet also pray to God as follows, wishing for pure and obedient offspring:

And who say: "Our Lord! Grant us that our spouses and offspring may be a means of happiness for us, and enable us to lead others in piety (to become a means of the promotion of piety and virtue). (Al-Furqan 25:74)

The desire for righteous and devout offspring in order to establish a family can be seen in many other verses and *hadith*s to be a part of establishing a family. In all such prayers and supplications, the purity, innocence, chastity, lack of sin, devotion, and belief of the generations are stressed. Therefore, the main issue regarding family is not the number of children, but rather each child's value before God, along with the depth of their belief and their submission to the foundations of faith.

## 3. Duties of the Father

a)  Measures to be taken before the birth of a child: Some of these measures are related to the preparation of housing, nutrition, clothing, and other material needs of the child.

b)  Nurturing and education: Naming the child, providing training and education to ensure the future livelihood of the child, in accordance with the age.

c)  Having a sense of responsibility in the nurturing and education of the child.

d)  Good examples being provided for the younger generation by the adults and the internalization of Islamic moral values within the family.

Now, let us examine these steps.

### a) Measures to be Taken before the Birth of Child

#### i) Cleanliness of the Seed

Sowing a seed on fertile soil and providing fresh air, clean light, pure water, and giving it the attention and care it needs while growing are important in the development of any plant. In the same way, providing a clean seed is an important prerequisite for the development of a healthy young generation. The following Prophetic tradition quoted in *Sahih al-Bukhari* and *Sahih Muslim* confirms this view. The Prophet is reported to have said: "He who is sinner is unfortunate in the womb; he who is fortunate is fortunate in the womb."[17]

Until the time when it can be decided whether or not the child is unfortunate or fortunate all necessary steps should be taken. From the moment of conception, the child's sustenance depends on the mother's actions. The attitude of the father and mother, before, during, and after conception, are important factors that determine the future of the child; these play a role as to whether the child will be fortunate or not.

It should be borne in mind that no reward will be given without our will and behavior being taken into consideration. The way we behave, the steps we take, and what these steps involve are all known by the Almighty Creator. In addition to these, our will and desires will also be taken into consideration and everything will be arranged accordingly. There are many children who are unlucky from the very moment they are born, due to the family environment into which they are born and the parents with whom they grow up. In some cases, God saves them and turn their lives into happy and pleasant ones, with His mercy and blessing.

The start of everything is the moment when the seed is sown, i.e. the moment of conception. The role of forbidden food and the sins of the parents cannot be underestimated in determining the nature of the child. If the seed is sown without the name of God being mentioned, whether the outcome of the pregnancy will be fortunate or not depends on God's blessing. Expecting a positive result from a bad start is very unrealistic. Yet, it is not impossible. As with Ikrimah, who was born into Abu Jahl's family, sometimes faithful people may come out of families with sinful life styles.

The following verse in the Qur'an indicates that, while on the one hand, some of the wishes of parents before the birth may come true, at the same time the parents should continue to wish and pray for a righteous child:

> When she grows heavy (with child), both (feel the need to) turn to God, their Lord, with prayer: "If You indeed grant us a righteous child, we will most certainly be among the thankful." (Al-A'raf 7:189)

---

[17] *Sahih Muslim*, "Qadar" 3; *Sunan ibn Majah*, "Muqaddima" 7; *Sahih al-Bukhari*, "Qadar" 1.

## ii) Sustenance should be Lawfully Earned

One of the duties of the parents is to be careful about the legitimacy of their own sustenance and to provide lawfully earned, legitimate, and untainted food for their children. As we have mentioned earlier that if a Muslim is in a position to provide unlawfully earned and religiously forbidden sustenance or doubtful food for his future family members, then the marriage of such a person is forbidden (*haram*) or abominable (*makruh*). No one has a right to feed others on religiously forbidden food.

We therefore have to provide lawfully earned sustenance and legitimate food for children and the other family members for whose nurture and care we are responsible. The fact that everyone else is partaking of forbidden or abominable food is not a justification for us to do the same. Even if times change, even if our society adopts new practices and everybody starts to act in illicit ways, we cannot feed our children with forbidden food. In fact, any unlawfully acquired sustenance or child whom we have nurtured with such food can one day cause us considerable distress, such as Hellfire, or perhaps inflict unbearable pain upon us.

If we have fully carried out our duties beforehand, than we can expect that our newly arrived guest will be a happy and contented person, protected to an extent from discomfort. However, if our sustenance, food, drink, and clothing have all been illicitly earned and our life is immersed in religiously forbidden things, then we wipe out the possibility of happiness for our child.

If we are living on unlawfully earned food and drink, this means that we are opening our spiritual world to the invasion of evil. "Evil moves in the veins of men alongside their blood"[18] the *hadith* goes. This indicates that evil floats in the veins of humanity contaminating the red and white blood cells, infecting our offspring and descendents.

To protect the unborn from such contamination, the care of the baby, its food, drink, and clothing must be provided for with legitimate means. From the very first day, the child should not be fed with unlawfully gained food nor should it be given water obtained in the same way, nor should it be dressed with illegitimately acquired clothing.

---

[18] *Sahih al-Bukhari*, "Ahkam" 21; "Bad'ul-Khalk" 11; "Itiqaf" 11, 12; *Sunan Abu Dawud*, "Sawm" 78; "Sunnah" 17, "Adab" 81; *Sunan ibn Maja*, "Siyam" 65.

A Prophetic tradition gives us the example of a man who is visiting the Ka'ba and uttering the blessed words of *labbayk Allahumma labbayk* (here we are O God, here we are at Your disposal); but at the same time he is dressed in unlawfully gained clothes and his stomach filled with forbidden food. The answer he receives from God will be *"La labbayka wa la sadayk"* (*"la"* in Arabic means "no"),[19] and his prayer is rejected.

We should not allow even one thread or one inch of a prohibited material to be found in our clothing. In case we use a prohibited material in our clothing without being aware of it, we should seek refuge in God and constantly fear Him in our hearts. It must be clearly understood that every seed we sow turns either into the poisonous *zaqqum* tree[20] or into a great and useful tree that contributes to the happiness of humankind, enduring for generations and aiding in the reconstruction of the earth, its roots going deep inside the earth, its branches towering in the sky, providing shade with its leaves and fruits for our nourishment.

## b) Education

One of the first responsibilities of a parent is to give a pleasant and meaningful name to their child, within the framework of the recommendations of the Messenger of God. The Prophet Muhammad, peace and blessings be upon him, attributed great importance to the naming of children. He is reported to have said: "Give the names of the Prophets. The most pleasant names before God are Abdullah and Abdurrahman. The most honest names are Kharis (literally means profit-bringing and winner of Heaven) and Humam (striving and resolute). The most unpleasant names are Harb (war, violence) and Murra (bitter, meanness)."[21] He also abolished such names as "Asiya," denoting rebellion, replacing it with "Jamila," which means beautiful.[22]

After the process of naming, legal procedure on breastfeeding[23] should be completed and question of providing child's sustenance and his/her education should be solved.

---

[19]  Al-Haythsami, *Al-Majma al-Zawaid*, 3/210; 10/292.

[20]  The tree mentioned in the Qur'an as being absolutely excluded from God's Mercy.

[21]  *Al-Musnad*, 4/345.

[22]  *Sahih Muslim*, "Adab" 14; *Sunan Abu Dawud*, "Adab" 66; *Sunan at-Tirmidhi*, "Adab" 62.

[23]  "Islam gives so much value to the breastfeeding relationship that any woman who nurses another's child in infancy is considered that child's legal foster mother. If

Every child is born with a pure nature.[24] A new born baby is like a blank sheet. You can write anything on this blank sheet; however you should only write those things that please God. This means that you nurture and cultivate the potentially good nature of the child. You are embossing on the personality of the child. What you teach should be valuable things that will weigh in their favor on the Day of Judgment before the angels and in the Hereafter. Such things should be in line with the direction that God and His Messenger have indicated.

It is the parents' responsibility to nurture, cultivate and educate a child at the correct time and in such a way that the impression of this remains forever on the soul of the child. Any couple who have children must devote some of each day to the cultivation and education of their children. We will deal with other aspects of nurture and education in the following chapters.

The family is the first school and the first academy in which the character is nurtured and where children are taught manners. The priority of the parents should be to teach manners and to educate their children. They should prefer devoting time to these activities rather than pursuing their personal duties. Important duties in the education of children are teaching about the existence of God and installing in the hearts of the children a belief in God, according to their age and their level of understanding. This is more important than the parent's material or spiritual feelings and takes precedent over the multiple personal duties of the parent. Therefore, if you go to Mecca on pilgrimage, yet leave behind you a rebellious child, your parental duties will call you back and say: "Where are you going, leaving such an important and critical duty behind?"

Additionally, a father should teach the child his or her religious beliefs, how to recite the Qur'an, and physical skills. He should not teach sports that utilize the power and energy of the brain merely to build

---

the same woman nurses other infants as well, the children are all considered "milk" brothers and sisters. Their bond is so close that they are considered to have the same relationship as blood siblings." *The Everything Understanding Islam Book: A Complete Guide to Muslim Beliefs*. Christine Huda Dodge. Avon: F+W Media. 2009, p. 113.

[24] *Sahih Al-Bukhari*, "Janaiz" 92; *Sunan Abu Dawud*, "Sunnah" 17; *Sunan at-Tirmidhi*, "Qadar" 5.

muscles, but rather all sports that contribute to leading a healthy life and that serve as some kind of introduction and preparation of the child for the future.

### c) A Sense of Responsibility in Nurturing

Quoting a reference which belongs to the Imamiyya school of thought, we would like to underline the significance of the responsibility in nurturing. Imam Zayn al-Abidin made the following recommendations in his book, entitled *Al-Risalat al-Huquq* (Treatise on Rights): "You should know that as the child is yours, any good or evil (that originates from him/her) will come back to you."

The Prophet Muhammad, peace and blessings be upon him, was given the ability to be aware of the approach of his own death before passing away. When he felt that his departure from this world was near, he unexpectedly said to his Companions: "There is a servant among the servants of God unto whom God has offered the choice between this world and that which is with Him, and the servant has chosen that which is with God." Abu Bakr, may God be pleased with him, who understood what was meant by this said: "Dearer than my father and my mother O the Messenger of God!" and then he began to cry.[25] He was quick to understand that the person who was to choose between this world and the Hereafter was the Prophet. Moreover, in his sermon during the Final (Farewell) Pilgrimage, the Prophet is reported to have said: "Soon they will ask you about me; did I do my duty of communicating the message of Islam properly? How will you reply?" He asked this question because, although he had carried out an important task, he was concerned as to whether or not he had done it properly. Yet, his performance was such that there was no doubt about how he had carried it out. Everybody in the audience called out in one voice and the following words resounded through the area: "You have done your duty, you have communicated your Prophethood and you have fulfilled your responsibilities properly." Then the Prophet raised his finger to heaven and said: "Be my witness, O God, that I have conveyed Your message to Your people."[26]

---

[25] *Sahih Muslim*, "Al-Fadail al-Sahaba" 1; *Sunan at-Tirmidhi*, "Manaqib" 15.
[26] *Sahih Muslim*, "Fitan" 8; "Hajj" 132; "Qasama" 31.

The Messenger of God was fulfilling an important responsibility that stretched over the Muslim community. He spoke of this responsibility with a deeply felt concern and asked for the testimony of his Companions. Now, can we ask the following question to the children who are under our responsibility, the children who we take care of: "They will ask you concerning me. How will you reply?" Are we confident of their answer? Can we expect them to answer "Yes, you have fulfilled your duties"? If the answer is "No," then we are in trouble. Concerning this issue, the great scholar Imam Zayn al-Abidin reminded us that "You will be questioned before God about how you have fulfilled your responsibilities towards your children." Then he made the following appeal to God: "Help me to nurture, educate, and do good deeds for my children." The most important and gravest task for a person is to enable his/her family to feel the joy of eternity by elevating them to a highest degree of perfection.

We sometimes buy presents for our children and try to please them. They are in our minds, even if we were on pilgrimage, when we are visiting the Ka'ba or even if we were to be in the presence of the Prophet. Even the most sacred and important duties cannot cause us to forget them. The most significant way reward our children are to instill in them the moral values of Islam and the good character of the Prophet. Nothing else that we can give is comparable to this gift; it enables them to experience eternal pleasure in the Hereafter. In this regard, the Prophet is reported to have recommended the following, found in a source of the Imamiyya school of thought: "Treat your children well and nurture them beautifully."[27] Nurturing and bringing up a child by reviving and following the way of the Prophet is the most precious gift that we can give.

### d) Setting a Good Example

Naturally, all parents of faith intend to raise their children as healthy and perfect members of an ideal society, the framework of which is defined according to the principles of the Qur'an. However, when parental intentions are not reflected in daily life or when they are not supported by ritual performances, such as daily prayer, pilgrimage, fasting and the paying of alms, then whatever the parents may say will have no influence on

---

[27] *Sunan ibn Majah*, "Adab" 3.

the children; if the parents' words are not backed up by good action or if the actions are not seen to be more effective than the words, then again, whatever the parents say will have no effect on the children. The parents may find that their words may even have the opposite effect of what is intended. Parents who wish for their words to have some influence on their children must first reflect the principles and practices which they want to instill in children in their own lives completely; only then can they expect their children to do the same thing.

Here I would like to mention a story, attributed to Imam Abu Hanifa, which sheds some light on this issue:

One day a child was brought to Imam Abu Hanifa and his father reported that honey was harmful for his boy. He said to the great Imam: "This child continues to eat honey, even though we tell him not to." Abu Hanifa asked them to take the child away and come back forty days later. The father brought the child back to the Imam forty days later. Imam then talked to the child and told him that he should not eat honey. When departing, the child kissed his father's hand and promised not to eat honey again. The people who were present asked the Imam: "Why didn't you tell him this when we brought him the first time; why did you make him wait for forty days?" Abu Hanifa answered them thus: "The day you brought the child to me I had eaten honey. If I had told him not to do something that I was doing, my advice would probably not have had any effect. I wanted a forty-day period in order to cleanse my body from the honey; only then could I give the child some advice."

Truthful words by themselves are not enough; it is important that one behaves in a proper manner as well. Any contradiction between our words and our behavior will shake our children's confidence in us. If your child discovers you have been lying or sees a contradiction between your words and your behavior just once, this is enough to make you unreliable in their eyes. As time goes on, this contradiction or lie will surface from the subconscious whenever you do something that makes the child even the least bit uncomfortable. Then the child will perceive you as a dishonest person and your words will have no effect on him or her. It is of utmost importance that our actions are carried out in such a way that our children should see us as an angel in the home, rather than a mere mortal father or mother. They should see in their parent gravity, devotion, responsiveness, and they should have complete trust in their parent. Parents who succeed in transmitting such feelings and thoughts in such a manner are the most successful teachers and instructors.

## 4. Parental Responsibility

Every person is responsible for a wide range of things, including one's family and one's children. All actions performed concerning the guardianship, protection and treatment of those for whom one is responsible will be recorded as good deeds. Failures in this regard will be recorded as wrongdoing.

God's Messenger is reported to have said the following *hadith*, cited in *Sahih al-Bukhari* and *Sahih Muslim*:

> Everyone of you is a guardian and everyone of you is responsible (for his wards). A ruler is a guardian and is responsible (for his subjects); a man is a guardian of his family and responsible (for them); a wife is a guardian of her husband's house and she is responsible (for it), a servant is a guardian of his master's property and is responsible (for that). Beware! All of you are guardians and are responsible (for your wards).[28]

The following *hadith* is also relevant to the issue discussed here, confirming that a child is entrusted to us: "Each child is born in a state of Islamic nature (*fitrah*).[29] But his parents make him or her a Christian, a Jew, or a Zoroastrian."[30]

Every child is in fact born with a pure innate ability and potential to become anything and everything. The child is then entrusted with a parent whose responsibility is to further develop his/her potential. That means that the nurturing and cultivation of the child is left to the parent. Later in their lives, a child can become a Christian, a Jew, or a Zoroastrian following in the footsteps of his/her parents. We should point out

---

[28] *Sahih al-Bukhari*, "Juma" 11; "Janaiz" 32; "Istiqraz" 20; "Wasaya" 9; "Itq" 17, 19; "Nikah" 81, 90; "Ahqam" 1; *Sahih Muslim*, "Imara" 20.

[29] When a child is born, it has with it a natural belief in God. This natural belief is called in Arabic the "*fitrah*." If a child were left alone, it would grow up aware of Almighty God in His Unity, but all children are affected by the pressures of their environment.

[30] *Sahih al-Bukhari*, "Janaiz" 80; "Tafsir" Sura (30) 1; "Qadar" 3; *Sahih Muslim*, "Qadar" 22, 23, 24.

here that some children may, despite their parents' religious orientation or that of their social environment, become an atheist or an apostate. Therefore, the religiosity and the devoutness of the parents are vital in the upbringing of children. Likewise, using religiosity and piety as the foundation for nurturing and educating children is very important.

It is a fact that if we do not raise our children according to our cultural and spiritual values, they will inevitably end up developing a personality that is alien to ours. You may become a father of an apostate, without even being aware of it. Therefore, in order to prevent our children from being alienated we must transmit the essence of our spirituality to them and instill in them its core values. In our orchards and vineyards we try to maximize the harvest by using all the latest technology to protect the trees. Are our children no less valuable? In the light of our values and principles are they less than wood, or stone? There is only one weapon with which our children can fight the two most serious of diseases, i.e., indifference which belittles everything and corruption which runs rampant; this is a weapon that only we, as parents, possess.

If we are not constructively involved in the education of our children, they will fall under the influence of others, and are in danger of being corrupted. Without positive intervention on our part, or if they fall under the influence of others, our children are in danger of being led down the path of degeneration. Parents of today have become absorbed in worldly affairs, leading them to completely neglect their children. There is no other time that we can look at where we can see children being as neglected as they are at this time.

The Prophet is reported to have said the following, according to another source of the Imamiyya school of thought: "What a pity for the children at the time when the end of the world is due, because of their fathers!" Upon hearing this statement, one of the Companions asked:

"Are they sacrificed because of their fathers, and then destroyed?"

"No, their fathers have sacrificed (destroyed) them," replied the Prophet.

He asked again: "How did that happen, O Messenger of God?"

"Their fathers did not teach them basic principles of religion," said God's Messenger.

This *hadith* may be interpreted as follows:

People have abandoned the basic principles of religion in favor of the short and trivial life of the material world. Those in a position of responsibility have completely neglected teaching and education, rather concentrating their attention on the material world exclusively. They have neglected the inner and spiritual world in order to gain temporary benefit in this trivial material world.

People do not care about teaching religious knowledge to children because, as far as they are concerned, teaching the Qur'an and instructing others in religion and spirituality take up too much time.

The following verse illuminates the above *hadith*:

Yes indeed! But you (people) love and prefer that which is before them (the present, worldly life); and abandon that which is to come later (the Hereafter) (Al-Qiyama 75:20–21).

The Messenger of God continues speaking as follows:

"I am far away from them; let them be far away from me."

Loosely interpreted, this means "I distance myself from those parents who have turned a blind eye to the corruption of their children, and also from those who are not afraid when they witness the destruction of a generation; I distance myself from them, let them stay away from me as well." I suppose fathers who are not spiritually dead will be frightened by these warnings; in fact they should tremble in fear when they hear this. When this important and weighty responsibility was explained to the Caliph Umar bin Abdulaziz, he fainted and could not be revived for a full twenty-four hours. Upon his having fainted, those around him thought that he had died, and therefore started to recite the Qur'an. When he came to himself, he told the people around him that he was afraid of God. He felt the heavy responsibility of his countrymen on his shoulders and worried terribly that he might have, in some way, violated their legal rights.

And what about us? How deeply should we fear and shake, neglecting our children's inner and spiritual lives having brought them into the family simply to satisfy our personal pleasures and desires?

The *hadith*s appear to emphasize principles that are both compassionate and terrifying in relation to child rearing. We must approach the issue under discussion from this perspective as well. There are a number of duties and responsibilities that Islam and the Qur'an impose upon us regarding the upbringing of our children and how we are to help shape their personalities. Earlier issues, given as principles, and the following points, that are to be explained in detail later, constitute important themes: Raising children as emotional, sensitive, well mannered and religious individuals; our being recognized as a respectable father or mother in our household; our building an image of ourselves as a wise person in our children's eyes, with fitting behavior, are all fairly important matters to be dealt with.

### a) Maintaining Equal Treatment among Children

The principle of treating our children equally and not preferring one of them above the others is primarily important. A minor error in this matter would be sufficient to nullify the effect of all that we say and do to our children. The following advice of the Prophet is very important:

Bashir, the father of Numan—both of them were Muslims and veterans of the battle of Badr—came to see the Prophet and said: "O Messenger of God! I have other children besides Numan. However if you were to allow it, I would like to hand over a portion of my property to Numan."

The Prophet asked: "Have you given each of your children the same amount?"

He said: "No."

Then the Prophet recommended the following, addressing himself to the public: "Fear God and treat your children with justice."

Turning to Bashir later on he asked: "Do you not want to see each of your children giving you equal respect?"

He said: "Yes."

"Then do not do this," said God's Messenger.[31]

This indicates that you should guard and take care of all of your children. If you are to concentrate your attention on only one of your children, if you prefer this child over the others and reward him/her by giving presents, then the other children's sense of respect towards you is lessened and their trust in you will be shaken.

The Prophet offered the ultimate solution to Bashir's problem. He solved it in a radical way. The preference of one particular child over the

---

[31] *Sahih al-Bukhari*, "Hiba" 12, 13; *Sunan an-Nasa'i*, "Nuhl" 1; *Sunan at-Tirmidhi*, "Ahkam" 30; *Sunan ibn Majah*, "Hiba" 1.

others in the family will lead, firstly, to the emergence of feelings of jealousy. Such behavior turns siblings against each other. Do not think that we are trying to explain this issue merely within the limited theories of psychology. Here we are elaborating the universality of the Qur'anic message; a message that this holy book conveys to our hearts and that is compatible with human nature, we are expounding its rationality, its acceptability, and its fundamental humanity.

As we know, the Prophet Joseph (Yusuf), peace be upon him, had a dream that the stars, the sun and the moon all prostrated themselves before him. When Joseph recounted this joyful dream to his father, his father replied, *"Do not relate your dream to your brothers"* (Yusuf 12:5). With his Prophetic vision and his depth of understanding, Joseph's father was well enough acquainted with human nature to see that such a delightful experience could be the cause of jealousy among the brothers. He thought that sharing this dream with the others could lead to rivalry in the hearts of those who had not achieved perfection in their inner lives, those who had not yet discarded their lower selves. Unfortunately, what he had feared eventually came about. Joseph's brothers threw him in a well, demonstrating the extent of corruption that jealousy can cause, even in the household of a Prophet.

Therefore, do not prefer one of your children over the others in matters of affection. It is clear that such preferential treatment stimulates feeling of jealousy among children and it will lead to a subconscious sense of hatred, caused by the parent's preferential treatment, even if those involved are not aware that such a thing is occurring.

It is easier to understand such ideas better if we contemplate our feelings of love and hatred, our friendships, and our hostilities in the light of their motivation and their subconscious roots. Let us imagine that we have a very close friend. Somehow this friend, one time, was unable to show the selflessness that we expect from a friend, and rather displayed unexpected selfishness. Consciously or unconsciously this experience is stored in a corner of your memory. Almost every event leaves a mark on the human memory, and latter another event will remind us of the previous one, bringing it back to the conscious level. In the face of an event that establishes an association with and awakens the unpleasant event that is sleeping in the subconscious, you all of a sudden become irritated and say, "I knew that you were this kind of person!"

Now, imagine that these unpleasant events build up and a few of them are brought together. All of these negative memories and unpleasant thoughts are brought to the fore, and you start to feel the need to defend yourself. In the same way, the preferential and unfair treatment of your children leads to the re-emergence of memories that are rooted in the subconscious of the child; such memories upset the child, eventually leading the child to be disobedient to you.

In fact, this is only one aspect of the matter. The problem becomes more complex if we approach the problem from the point of view of the entire life of a person. If you attribute every misbehavior as being due to childishness, rather than considering the child's feelings and dealing with the problem on that level, all of this will build up, developing into bigger problems in the future; one day you will be crushed under the insurmountable accumulation of mistakes, mistakes of which you were totally unaware. Inconsistent behavior or words and acting in a way that contradicts your words, things which you assume that a child cannot understand, all leave an indelible mark on their memory. When the time is right, all of these will suddenly surface. The re-emergence of such things may occur in such a powerful way that it will sweep away the father and mother.

Anyone who desires to become a parent should have a basic understanding of pedagogy and psychology, or at least they should be aware of the general principles found in the Qur'an that pertain to this issue.

Child rearing is not a simple matter. Once I became interested in beekeeping. In order to find out more, I took courses in beekeeping. I realized how difficult it was to deal with these small creatures. In the same way, human beings should learn methods of how to bring up good generations and how to deliver useful members of society. Nobody should ever forget how important it is to nurture a great being, a being with the potential to move between the lowest and the highest stations of spirituality, a being that has the ability to elevate itself to the level of humanity.

## b) Taking Children Seriously

God's Messenger put great emphasis on the importance of children. He would listen to them as if they were grownups; he would carry them on his shoulders, sit them in his lap, or cradle them in his arms. He used to treat them all as equals and would make efforts to please them.

He used to greet children whenever he saw them playing, treating them as if they were grown ups.[32] If the Messenger of God promised a child that he would give them something at a given time, he always kept his promise, just the same as if he made a contract with an adult.

### c) Instilling a Sense of Trust

The maxim "Trust no one, not even your father" is one of the most disgraceful attitudes of modern society; this is a very grave error. God's Messenger always inculcated the idea of "trust" and the children who grew up around him knew him, first and foremost, as someone to trust. He was a trustworthy person for all who knew him. Naturally, if a society or a nation were to be composed of trustworthy individuals, then this society also would be reliable. The Messenger of God always advised to be sensitive and loving to children: "God will not be merciful to those who show no compassion to their children."[33]

He would underline the most important points of nurturing a child. He recommended to his Companions that they love their children and that they keep any promises made. He used to remind them not to give children any opportunity to see contradictions between their words and their actions.

God's Messenger is reported to have said the following, again found in a source attributed to the Imamiyya school of thought: "If any of you make a promise to his/her child, you should keep that promise at all costs." Here we can see that the attitude, held by many, that "Oh, they are just children, it doesn't matter if I don't keep my word" is completely incorrect.

Any lies or words which contradict the truth will leave seeds in a child's memory and these seeds will grow, maybe now, maybe in the future, into the poisonous *zaqqum* tree, rendering all educational efforts void. Parents must follow the straight path. It is of utmost importance

---

[32] *Sunan Abu Dawud*, "Adab" 135, 136; *Sunan ibn Majah*, "Adab" 14.
[33] Al-Haythami, *Al-Majma al-Zawaid*, 8/155.

that, as people on the straight path, your words and behavior should only contain the truth.

You must not allow for an opportunity to arise in which your children may think or say that you have lied, or that you have not kept your promise, or that you have acted in a selfish manner. They should see you as always reliable, devout, faithful, patient, God-fearing, and virtuous, and as one who is selfless in putting others before yourself.

### d) A Gradual Method of Nurturing

Children should be instructed in the issues that they need to know and they should not be instructed in matters which are of no use. Children should be informed of things that are necessary for the development of their mental and spiritual life in a way that is suitable for their age level. We will elaborate on this issue in detail in the following chapters.

In order to get information about the physical development of our child, we go to a doctor and ask which food should be given to the child and we program the baby's diet according to this expert's advice. In the same way, we should seek expert opinion concerning the education and nurturing of our children, according to their developmental levels.

In fact, every mother and father should learn the principles and methods of raising children from experts in the field and they should try to educate their children accordingly. If your child has a high-school education, it is not enough to simply tell him/her that "God exists," without providing any evidence or arguments. If you were to display such an attitude you may push this person to reject the existence of God altogether. At this period and age, religious knowledge should be presented to children intertwined with some philosophical arguments, allowing our opinions to have an impact on this young person. However, if you start teaching your child philosophy lessons while they are still in primary school, you will only succeed in totally confusing them. Rather, you should, like a pediatrician, cultivate your children and teach them, taking into consideration their level of understanding, the time they live in, and their social environment.

Chapter Three

---

AWARENESS IN EDUCATION

# AWARENESS IN EDUCATION

If your family is based on a framework that pleases Almighty God and His Messenger, then it is a promising one. In other words, if the children you raise proceed along a path that follows the Prophet, then their future is bright and you can think yourself successful. On the contrary, if the children you raise wander the streets, if they grow up anti-religious and hostile towards the mosque and the prayers, they will be doomed to unhappiness and you can consider yourself as being responsible. Such an outcome is an injustice, first to your children and also to society. No one has the right to commit such a grave injustice. We will be accountable for raising children that are hostile to Islam, for children who consume unlawfully earned and forbidden food and drink and for children who breach our social rules with objectionable behavior. It is one of our greatest duties to raise children who have a sense of spiritual mission; such children will be far-sighted and compassionate and will respect their fellow human beings. In short, this vital duty is one that begins consciously with the establishment of a family and is sustained throughout life with the use of reason, logic, and discernment.

The family should be perceived as being an institution that is built on the foundation of the spirit of religion, reason, and awareness. The family should be maintained according to the principles of pleasing Almighty God. The Prophet Muhammad, peace and blessings be upon him, stated that he would be made proud by the quantity of his followers. However, no generation is valuable before God, no matter its size, if it does not recognize Him. Neither will such a generation have a value for the Messenger of God.

Therefore, we should eradicate the roots of negative tendencies by turning to God, asking for forgiveness with sincere regret, on the one hand, while continuing to be actively hopeful through prayers and good deeds, initiatives that contribute to positive tendencies, and by constantly turning to God and fulfilling whatever physical, emotional, or verbal responsibilities are necessary, on the other.

In this context, the Qur'an reveals the following:

> Say (O Messenger): "The bad and the good are not alike," even though
> the abundance of the bad (the sheer quantity of the corrupt) amazes you.
> So keep from disobedience to God in reverence for Him and piety, O peo-
> ple of discernment (so that you may rightly distinguish quality and quan-
> tity, and so), that you may prosper (in both worlds). (Al-Maedah 5:100).

As a matter of fact, the amount of evil and villainy in the world may
surprise you. However, you should be aware of the fact that evil and
good have never been equal before God. Thus, you should always be
aware of the importance of raising a generation that reminds you of Paradise with their spiritual radiance, while trying to follow the "good" and
trying to become a "good" parent, educator, and instructor.

## 1. The Illness of *Wahn* (Love for the World and Fear of Death)

God's Messenger is reported to have said the following in an authenti-
cated *hadith*: "In the future, people will flock around you like a hungry
person rushes to dinner table; they will try to grab the food from your
mouth." What we can understand from this is that people will crowd
in on you, stealing your wallets, and taking your property, just like
people crowding around a dinner table. One of his Companions asked
him. "Would such a thing happen because our population is so small,
O Messenger?" The Prophet answered his Companion as follows: "No,
on the contrary you will be extremely numerous on that day; but God
will root out the love felt towards you from the heart of your enemies;
(i.e. you will not be esteemed people before your enemies, you will not
be able to give assurances and make others feel your power and importance). At the same time God will place *wahn* (love of world and fear
of death) in your hearts."

The same Companion asked again: "What does *wahn* mean, O Messenger of God?"

The Prophet is reported to have said, "*Wahn* means the love of
worldly life (with its temporary aspects), giving priority to this life and
fear of death."[34]

---

[34]  *Sunan Abu Dawud*, "Malahim" 5; *Musnad*, 2/359; 5/278.

In fact, if a society perceives the conquest of the world as being its main target, a conquest that consists of several dimensions that serve the lower self, and if society internalizes this aim in its heart and soul, then this society will no longer have a spiritual direction, even if its members profess the oneness of God (*La ilaha illallah*). This will be true for as long as the members of this society continue to abandon pleasing God and prefer the material world and whatever is present there to Him. It is this that the Messenger of God is speaking about when he says, "God will place *wahn* in your hearts."

In summary, it should be our primary aim to raise a generation that has a strong faith and formidable will, a generation committed to not giving into the temporary attractions of the world, a generation that has no place in its heart for the love of this world or the fear of death, a generation who stands strong against its enemies.

## 2. The Woman's Role

The Prophet Muhammad, peace and blessings be upon him, is reported to have said, "Almighty God is never angrier than when He is angry concerning the negligence of the rights of women and children", i.e. what angers God most is the condition of women and children.

A generation that has willfully surrendered itself to sins and has become wretched and enslaved by its worldly desires invites the wrath of God. The first and foremost duty of the head of every family is to choose his companion (wife) from among Muslim, faithful, loyal, patient, pious[35], trustworthy, and devout[36] women. A companion is a friend for life and is also a pious teacher with whom one can discuss every issue; this is an essential requirement for people to achieve worldly and spiritual happiness. Indeed, it is very important to have a spouse with an understanding mind and heart, so that one can reveal one's innermost spiritual and worldly feelings. It is vital to provide an atmosphere and a home where children will be raised under the supervision of a mother who is a teacher and an instructor.

---

[35] See Al-Ahzab 33:35.
[36] *Sahih Muslim*, "Rada" 59; *Sunan ibn Maja*, "Nikah" 5.

## 3. Giving Priority to the Inner Profundity

The Qur'an explains how insignificant quantity and plenitude are as follows:

> God has already helped you on many fields, and on the day of Hunayn, when your multitude was pleasing to you, but it availed you nothing, and the earth, for all its vastness, was too narrow for you, and you turned back, retreating. (At-Tawba 9:25).

God's Messenger led the battle of Hunayn following the conquest of Mecca. In the first instance, the Muslims could not fight as well as they had previously against the forces of Hawazin. On this day, as the Qur'an points out, the Muslims thought that "nobody could withstand the forces of this army," and they depended heavily on Divine assistance. However, when they came face to face with the archers of the Hawazin forces, they could not help but feel surprised by the turn events took. As this episode shows, a plenitude of numbers is not everything, even if this is what the Companions thought.

In fact, what is important is quality and profundity. As the Companions were more faithful to God, this temporary shock, and retreat was a sin for them; but not for us. What is emphasized in this verse of the Qur'an is that at no place and in no time will number and quantity be of any importance. Muslims should submit their will to and place emphasis on inner profundity and quality rather than plenitude of numbers, no matter where they live. These should all be attributed to God.

You will achieve success with the help of God if you submit yourself to God and convey the Divine messages to others with unflagging enthusiasm, even if your numbers are few or you are in a weak state. If, instead, you remain within the confines of your home and forget your relationship with God, your numbers will mean nothing, no matter how great.

## 4. Your Duties towards Your Children

### a) Preparing an Atmosphere for Education

To ensure the best education of our children, we must also generate the best educational atmosphere. Every child is molded according to his/her environment; in a sense a child is the product of the atmosphere that he/

she lives in. The family is the primary educational environment, followed by the school and friends and peers.

If you do not properly prepare your children for the environment into which they will venture and if you fail to develop their abilities then inevitably your children will one day "catch a virus". In fact, a child who grows up in an unsuitable environment will, without doubt, one day become corrupted. Therefore, starting with your family, you must prepare a proper environment for every stage and part of life to ensure the perfect education for your child; once things go wrong you cannot turn back the clock.

### b) Refraining from Feeding Unlawfully Earned or Forbidden Foods

It is extremely important to feed a baby, starting from the moment of conception and during the embryo stage, with legitimately earned and permissible food and drink. We must definitely keep in mind that any interruption in the connection of the child with God during the child's developmental stages may have a negative impact—even if just temporarily—on the child's personality. This is a common occurrence. An unlawful or forbidden morsel in the mother's veins—and the same goes for the father as well—may later turn out to be a cause of temporary or permanent corruption.

### c) Protection from "Evil and Malicious Eyes"

It is important to protect a child from evil and malicious eyes after his birth as much as you try to protect him from illegitimate food, drink, and nutrition.

You should absolutely take into account that corrupted, dirty minded, bad worded, sinful, and wicked eyes may damage some of the subtle spiritual senses of a child.

These are among the duties towards your child which you should fulfill as an expression of your relations with God and religion. If we fulfill these duties with great care, we may become a society like a community of angels.

## d) Organizing the Family Environment

The Messenger of God is reported to have said, "The first word a child utters should be *La ilaha illallah* (There is no deity but God)."[37]

Naturally the first word a child utters, at the age of two, should be "mummy" or "daddy"; what we should try to encourage the first word to be is "God (Allah)"[38] because God is eternal. Then, having established this solid base, at a later stage other concepts can be added on, concepts such as love, respect, and freedom according to his age and level of comprehension. If the child is in primary education then he or she needs to be given information directed at this level. If the child is attending high school, and reading philosophy and social and human sciences then he or she will need to receive information from sources in these fields.

If there is respect for God and if He is frequently the subject of discussion in a house, then we have focused on the target of motivating our children to utter their first willful word as we would wish. In fact, in a family setting there should be people praying, inclining, and rising in the rhythm of their daily prayers; in short, there should be a feeling of awe before God in the family setting. In such a family atmosphere, everything is in order, and there is constant discussion of God, making it easier for the child to utter the word "God" as his or her first word.

## e) Setting the Dose of Fondness

We should not—God forbid—display a love for our children that is in excess of the love we feel for God. Our love for our child, as deep as it is, should not be equal to nor exceed our love for God.

If we love our child to the extent that we love God, we may, inadvertently, be attributing a partner to God, and thus be engaged in a form of polytheism. There is no doubt that it would be an enormous mistake to excessively love our child to the degree that we forget God in the process. Moreover, such an excessive love will cause you to display behavior that is not under control, and this is harmful for the child. When people speak of "forbidden love" before God, it is assumed that they are speaking of this type of uncontrolled love. When you show the love that

---

[37] Abd al-Razzaq, *Musannaf*, 4/334.

[38] Al-Haythami, *Al-Majma al-Zawaid*, 8/159.

should be directed towards God to a human being then you may damage the relation between you and God.

Moderation in love is important for the following reasons:

1. The Lord of our heart is Almighty God. No other love should replace love for God in our hearts.

2. We must be in no doubt that our children are God's entrusted gifts. The love and compassion that we feel for these children is a kind of bonus and a helping hand that is given to us to help make looking after this entrusted being easier. In fact, your love for this child is a gift given to you by God, who is the Most Compassionate and the Provider. Love and compassion are given to you so that you can look after the child entrusted to you in the best possible manner.

### f) Setting a Good Example

Your aim, when dealing with the child that you are responsible for raising, your emotions, thoughts, words, spiritual life and behavior, should always be to set a good example. If you want your children to grow up in the best possible way, then you have to give the utmost attention to this matter. For example, if you want to see your children praying, then you must set them a good example by praying in such a way that they can see you and emulate you. You should make clear your attitude regarding the limits of decency before God. You should always tell the truth, and avoid lying at all costs. If you do not wish for them to speak badly or to swear, then you should refrain from doing the same. If you want them to become decent people and to lead an honest life, respecting the chastity and decency of others, then you have to provide a suitable environment in the home and you yourself should be the first example of such behavior. If you want them to recite the Qur'an and develop an understanding of the truths contained within it, you should then discuss the issues contained in the Qur'an day and night, allowing your children to listen to your discussions. You should show great respect for the Qur'an, so that you do not push your children in the opposite direction.

In summary, the most effective means of education are words, emotions, spiritual passion and proper behavior and there is no question that these should be employed in the education of children. If you just hire someone else to educate your child and tell this person to "teach a few things to my child," you will never reach your child, and will be unable to teach him or her anything.

## g) Enabling Children to Develop a Sense of Appreciation and a Love for God

Children are not required to perform the compulsory prayers when they are of primary school age, and sometimes even a little bit later. Any mistakes made concerning prayers at this age are not the subject of discipline. Children should never be disciplined or punished at this time for any such errors.

However, you must always remember that whatever you teach a child at this age, that is, at an age before a child is responsible, will remain in his or her mind and heart throughout life. This is why we need to improve and consolidate their sense of appreciation. They should be made aware of the blessings they have received and should thank God and people in return for His blessings and for their favors.

Their sense of appreciation and thankfulness will deepen with time and this child will become a person who offers praise to God in return for His blessings, while also being thankful to the people around him when they do good deeds. In fact we have to improve the innate desire in our child to perform good deeds and to appreciate the performance of the same by others so that they will be able to successfully comprehend the concept of God. Finally, a person who has received such an education will be able to profess the greatness of God while appreciating the favors done by other people. In time, the appreciative behavior of such a person will become so ingrained as to become a personality trait. Thus such a person will always say "thank you" for every blessing.

Another important point to be made here is that we should tell our children about God's kindness, blessings, and His beneficence; in short we should inform them of all the things which make us rejoice. We should help to consolidate a sense of trust, belief and love in our children by explaining to them how God feeds us, how He nurtures us, how He sustains us, and how He keeps us alive. We should inform our children about how God shows His affection to us and how He protects us from evil and disaster. Furthermore, we should improve our children's relations with God, helping them to make a connection by explaining to them, in a suitable language, that even the smallest beings in the universe can survive, thanks merely to His kindness and blessings.

Through this educational process the universe will emerge in the mind of our children as an entity that is continuously remembering God's attributes of Beneficence and Mercy. The fact that there is a provider for every blessing will resound through our house; the consciousness of our children will be filled with a sense of appreciation for the Provider of all blessings. Our house will be like a sanctuary for offering thanks.

However, in all these matters our children should be addressed in a manner appropriate to their age, as follows:

> If He did not give, the pomegranate tree would not bear fruit
> Animals would not produce milk if He were not the owner
> No drop of rain would come from sky without His mercy
> Nor would grass grow on earth if He were not merciful
> If He were not to will it we would not be able to talk
> If He were not to enable us, we would not be able to see
> If He were not to will it so we would not be able to hear
> Our thirst would not be quenched
> Our organs would not function,
> If He were not to will it so
> Indeed He is the Master and Owner of all these, my child
> We have not created them; everything comes from Him
> And everything is under His custody and surveillance.
> Therefore my child, He will increase these blessings
> If our heart overflows with love for Him,
> For He, Who prepared and gave these blessings to us.
> But, if we are ungrateful
> He will cease to give them to us
> He will deprive us of their benefits
> He will take them from us (see Ibrahim 14:7).

Such a method functions as a form of rehabilitation. We can convey all these messages and principles to our children through our behavior, our words, our looks, and our emotions.

## h) Communicating through the Language of Attitude

The most effective way to train and educate is reflected in our manners and behavior. There is no doubt that the proper organization of family life will start children thinking.

You cannot possibly imagine how much your children witnessing you praying in the middle of the night (*tahajjud*) can influence and contribute to their unconscious growth. If your child sees you praying at this time, it will inspire him or her. The child asks himself why you are crying, why you are being emotional, and why you are experiencing heartfelt pain while you pray. If he or she asks these things within the family, you should tell your child that you feel awe when before God and fear at being deprived of His blessings and having to face torment. Along with these worries, express with hope and affection that you respect God and emphasize that you are under His supervision and care. You need to make your child understand the life style that you have set for yourself and the inner profundity that you feel. If you try to explain to your child things that have not yet taken root in your heart and soul or things that you do not internalize, you will not be able to instill a sense of trust, nor exercise any influence on the child.

It is reported that Aisha, may God be pleased with her, was asked the following: "What kind of morality did the Messenger of God possess?" She replied, "Don't you read the Qur'an? His morality was the morality of the Qur'an."[39]

Drawing upon the message of this Prophetic tradition we can understand the moral position of the Prophet Muhammad, peace and blessings be upon him, as follows: God's Messenger had a life style and a form of living which are explained in the Holy Qur'an.

As a matter of fact, when the Prophet brought the message of the Qur'an to us, he conveyed a message that he had already internalized and made into a life style. There was a living Qur'an (a message embodied in the personality of the Messenger) and a life to be read. It was for this reason that the message he transmitted with his words and exemplary behavior made an impact on pure consciences and was accepted by all. People accepted this message and tried to put it and its principles into action.

---

[39] *Sahih Muslim*, "Musafirin" 139; *Sunan ibn Majah*, "Ahkam" 14; *Musnad*, 6/91.

Therefore, our behavior and words should not contradict one another. If there is no harmony between our actions and our words this is behavioral hypocrisy. Differences between our inner world and our external conduct will lead a child to hypocrisy, paradoxes, and dual perceptions. Such a contradiction makes a child waver (*muzabzab*)[40] between different views.

When you explain to a child the blessings of God, he or she will accompany you in turning to Him with a sense of appreciation and thankfulness. The child will utter the following: "Praise be to God for the thousands of times that you have talked about Him; praise be to the One that created and made us human, Who has blessed us with endless bounties, endowed us with health, given us parents, bestowed on us different food everyday, has created the air, the water, the soil and the trees and Who has granted their use to us."

If you try to instill these views and continue to lead discussions at home on these lines then everything will attain a separate beauty. There is an exceptional place for compassion in educating and nurturing a child. It is reported that the Messenger of God treated his personal assistants with such a kindness that his compassion surpassed parental affection.

It is related that Anas ibn Malik, may God be pleased with him, reported the following event: "I served God's Messenger for ten years; I do not remember him saying "Why did you not do it?" when I had not done something I was supposed to have done. Nor do I remember him saying "Why did you do it?" when I had done something that I was not supposed to have done. He never disciplined me nor treated me unpleasantly."[41] In fact, he treated people with such tenderness and kindness and dealt with them much better than their own parents could have done. He was extremely kind and compassionate towards his own children and grandchildren. Only he could be transcendental to such a degree.

### i) Compassion

If children must fear something let it be a fear of the loss of their parents' compassion rather than physical punishment, or threats or pain. If a

---

[40] See An-Nisa 4:143. *Muzabzab* means one who is unsteady.
[41] *Sahih al-Bukhari*, "Adab" 39; *Sahih Muslim*, "Fadail" 13; *Sunan at-Tirmidhi*, "Birr" 69.

frown on the father's face and displeased expression on the mother's are perceived as the greatest sanctions, and if these will put the child back on the right track, then this is enough, maybe even more than enough, of a discipline. However, your children's trust in you and their belief that you share their pains and suffering are extremely important. Therefore, when they cry you should also cry, if possible, or at least you should try to share their pain. You should express your sorrow and share their pain when children suffer, just as heaven grieves for the dead.[42] In this way, your status will be higher before them and your words will exercise more influence on them. You will enter their hearts in such a way that they will never be able to uproot you from there. All your words will make an impact on their hearts and minds.

If you want them to grow like angels and if you expect them to represent you perfectly in the future, then this supreme goal can only be achieved through these methods.

## j) Authority

It is of vital importance that there should not be a lack of authority at home. If there is no authority to ensure harmony, the family will suffer from disorder and the children will fall into a dilemma. Regarding authority, responsibility, and order, the Qur'an prescribes the following:

> Men (those who are able to carry out their responsibilities) are the protectors and maintainers of women inasmuch as God has endowed some of people (in some respects) with greater capacity than others, and inasmuch as they (the men) spend of their wealth (for the family's maintenance). Good, righteous women are the devoted ones (to God) and observant (of their husbands' rights), who guard the secrets (family honor and property, their chastity, and their husband's rights, especially where there is none to see them, and in the absence of men,) as God guards and keeps undisclosed (what should be guarded and private). As for those women from whose determined disobedience and breach of their marital obligations you have reason to fear, admonish them (to do what is right); then, (if that proves to be of no avail), remain apart from them in beds; then (if that too proves to be of no avail), beat them lightly (without beating them in their faces). Then, if they obey you (in your directing them to observe God's rights and their marital obliga-

---

[42] The great universe is related to the little universe. Perhaps, if a Muslim feels sorry, the universe of grace feels equally sorry. In this way, the sorrow is shared.

tions), do not seek ways against them (to harm them). (Be ever mindful that) God is indeed All-Exalted, All-Great. (An-Nisa 4:34).

Man is responsible for establishing order and harmony on specific issues in the home. It can further be argued that he has the uppermost responsibility in most issues. It is well-known that children need such a responsible figure around. A child who witnesses a sense of responsibility being displayed openly in the home will not lead a disorganized and irresponsible life. On the contrary, the presence of two irresponsible people and two different types of order coming from two opposing sides will only confuse a child.

In fact, children should be able to take refuge in either their fathers or in their mothers if they become frightened of the other parent. The natural place to take refuge should be in the mother's arms. If the roles are shared in the traditional manner, the children will observe discipline and authority in the father, while in the mother they will find tenderness and compassion and thus, although they will be frightened at times they will also be hopeful, and will never feel lonely. If this is not how the family life is, i.e. if family life has not been established on such a union and there is no division of labor, then the contradictions will continue. Children will grow up insensitive, cruel, rough, and without a sense of direction; they will have been brought up in a family environment where the mother is the leader in her own right with the father being a leader going off in a different direction.

In our opinion, in order to raise healthy generations there must be an ideal home environment. Therefore, a family or a home should first of all be linked to God. If the parents, or even one of them, are to approach the daily issues of the family in the role of God's vice-regent, then the family members will become righteous, honorable, and cognizant of the important issues to the same degree as they are submissive to God. No serious problems will exist in such a family atmosphere.

## 5. Adopting God's Morality

### a) Manner of Speech

The first issue that needs to be dealt with here is adopting and internalizing higher moral values and the supreme ethical principles that have a

Divine source. All our thoughts, behavior and even our discussions with our spouse should constantly be centered on issues that we think will enter the unconscious thought of the child.

Naturally, you will talk and discuss other matters in the home. But when you discuss matters in the presence of your child, you should pay special attention to the fact that he or she is there. If possible, issues which do not concern children and which are not constructive for them should not be discussed in their presence. Discussions of problems that would be depressing to children should be avoided. Children should not be exposed to problems which are beyond their capacity to bear and issues that may make an impression, negative or otherwise, on their minds and hearts should be carefully considered. When children are around, conversations, debates and discussions, either at home or in the office, should be conducted with their presence being taken into account.

Any discussions or conversations conducted in the presence of children should center on God, our faith in Him, on His blessings and on religion, to the greatest extent possible. As a principle, you should discuss only issues, values and principles that you want your children to emulate in the future, so that children grow up being aware of what their primary concerns should be. If we take on board these suggestions and recommendations as a prescription for a healthy life, an important proportion of the problems children face will be eliminated. There will of course be other problems that arise in the future; when the time comes these will also be discussed.

### b) Moderation in Mercy and Compassion

Another issue we would like to discuss here is the development of a sense of mercy and compassion in our children and the need to raise them as heroes of compassion. The most effective and short-term method is, again, to set a good example and to present this quality to children in their home environment. For example, if both parents were to rush to the aid of another and to listen to this person's problem with compassion when they come asking for help, this will have a great impact on inculcating a sense of kindness and compassion in our children.

A sense of compassion passes from parents to children. For example, some children cry easily as compared to others, even when they are very young. This state is a sign that this child will be a sensitive and emotional person later in life. However, some children pretend to be crying simply because they either want to gain the attention of their parents or they want to achieve a goal. Yet cries that come from sensitivity and tenderness are always different. If we want our children to be generous, tender, and compassionate, then we should provide a warm, delicate, and compassionate family environment for them.

An education that raises a child as a mean and self-centered person, a person who is fond of material things, sets the pattern for this child, under the right conditions, to become selfish, egocentric, aggressive, and rebellious. If a child has not been raised to follow the principles and values of Divine morality, then such training will have unfortunate consequences in his or her latter life in this world and in the Hereafter.

In fact, mercy and compassion are extremely important. Generosity and benevolence are expressions of such states of spirituality. Heroes of compassion are always the winners and merciless ones are always the losers. Generous people can enter Paradise, even if they have caused some problems occasionally. The chances of an ungenerous person entering Paradise are very slim, even if such a person has faith. Therefore, a sense of compassion and sympathy must be developed in our children; their sense of charity and willingness to help should be enhanced so that they will not succumb to this world and forget other human beings, becoming lost in the material world. You should teach your children how to give to charity; they will then give to charity when they are older, following the path to God with their hearts, souls, and minds. It needs to be said once again that any efforts to instill the idea of charity will not be effective if not supported by words and deeds. When we explain issues with our behavior, i.e. by setting examples, then our words will be as effective as the breath of an angel.

## c) Rewards

The other issue which should be taken into account is rewarding our children in proportion to their achievements. I particularly use the term "proportion" here because it is more correct to give a larger reward for a more significant success, i.e. in proportion to its importance, and a small reward for a minor achievement, according to the principles of justice.

In fact, it is a requirement of Divine morality to reward every achievement, whether it is related to religious matters or whether it is concerned with this world.

From this perspective, "parents" are thinkers, sages, and educators to some extent. They should try to understand, think carefully, and protect their children with great care. It is obvious that children will not have very refined senses and thoughts if the parents do not show or give as much importance to their children as they do to their home and property.

We need to return to the fundamental source once again to find principles concerning children in all situations. This fundamental source is Divine morality. In the Hereafter, God promises Paradise as a reward for those who have done good deeds and punishment for those who have done bad deeds in this world. Regarding this promise, the Qur'an has the following to say,

> And (remember also) when your Lord proclaimed: "If you are thankful (for My favors), I will most certainly give you more; but if you are ungrateful, surely My punishment is severe. (Ibrahim 14:7)

We should display such a measured and careful attitude to a child who has adopted Divine morality so that God will not condemn us to loneliness.

## d) Preparing Your Child for the Future

There is also one final point which is useful to mention in this context. It is the fact that children should be treated and inculcated by taking into account their social environment, age, and educational and cultural background. If a child is five years old, then the religious information we will transmit and teach him or her should be chosen according to his or her understanding, just as we provide age-appropriate food and nutrition. Likewise, when the same child is seven, we need to chose different information and when he or she is ten we have to re-arrange once again what will be taught at this age level.

Nevertheless, there is an important issue here concerning what we do teach. Whatever we teach should not be concerned with the child's age and time, but rather with the forthcoming period. Children will learn and understand their own age by experiencing it. In this regard, what they are taught by their teachers and peers may be sufficient. Therefore, the level at which we will try to teach them moral education should be one level higher than what they learn from school and from their immediate surroundings.

Ali ibn Abu Talib, may God be pleased with him, is reported to have said, *"You should teach your children not the knowledge and culture of your present age but manners and morals of the next age; children were created to live not in your time but for a different period."* If this principle is interpreted from the perspective of general knowledge and culture, one can argue that confining oneself to present information and learning is shortsighted, and others will leave you behind if you do not move ahead. When this principle is applied to the field of child education, it would be more beneficial to follow an educational course that moves beyond the present age and takes the future into account. In fact, a child should be exposed to an education suitable for seven when he is six and an education suitable for eight when he is seven.

In summary, the following can be said: The level of religious moral education to be given to a child at the age of five should be continued and advanced stage by stage until the child reaches puberty. The educational issues and materials should be chosen carefully, according to the age level of the child, so that such matters will not cause any problems for the understanding of the child. A child should be able to absorb what you are teaching. If you try to educate a fifteen-year old at the comprehension level of a twenty year old person, you will turn the young person's world upside down and cause confusion in his or her religious understanding, faith, and moral values. Just as everyone needs different food or drink for nutrition, due to their genetic and physical differences, the mind, emotions, consciousness, understanding, and heart also need to be fed in accordance with the level of development.

If you attempt to teach a number of things to someone who is under your care without understanding his or her social, intellectual, and mental level, and capacity, you push them away from you emotionally. It is a blessing from God that some young people have managed to still have sound and strong faith and emotions, despite being given incorrect education and taught faulty practice. In some cases, people who have suffered this have had their intellectual and mental capabilities underdeveloped. If that is the case that means that such people are living at the level of a fifteen-year old and they are living much behind their own time, despite their age. Such a person may inevitably experience a crisis of faith and may reject his or her own religion if one day he or she comes across a religious, social theory, or idea that is above his or her level of comprehension.

Religion makes the following recommendations regarding the provision of an education suitable to the age of children, or maybe one that is a little advanced: If performing prayers is compulsory for a child at the age of fifteen, you should then teach him or her to pray at the age of ten. Similarly, you should teach children to fast before this duty becomes compulsory, allowing time for them to become accustomed to it. This principle can be extended to all other issues which mold the child according to his age.

I would like to point out that our unfaltering statements regarding value judgments here stem from the fact that our approach to this issue is drawn from perspectives of the Qur'an and the Prophetic traditions and our strong beliefs are related to this. We believe that the education and training of children should start at an early age, exposing them to teaching when they are still young. This is a more effective method. If we wish for them to be performing compulsory religious duties when they have reached an age of discernment, then we should teach the required duties and prayers much earlier. We have witnessed the positive outcomes of such an approach many times.

Here I would like to mention some of the characteristics and traits belonging to certain ages, drawing upon the views of Imam Jafar: The period of childhood lasts until the age of seven. A child imitates whatever he sees and his life is carried out playing different games. You play with the child and enjoy it; the child also enjoys playing with you. He or she learns whatever you do and imitates it. His or her life consists almost entirely of play and imitation during this period. After this age, the period of inculcation, according to the level of understanding, follows. In this period, we should help the child through an inculcation process and then motivate him or her to learn and internalize our spiritual values, according to his or her level of comprehension and capability of understanding. This is the period of studying the revealed word of God, i.e.

the Qur'an; this is something that requires much time. After this a period of understanding what is prohibited and what is allowed begins; this is also something that requires much time.

According to the theory and method of Imam Jafar, the religious and social development of a person should be complete by the time they reach the age of twenty-one. What is implied here is that it will not be so easy to teach a person new things concerning values and the spiritual aspects of life after this age. Therefore, a person should be inculcated and educated concerning religious matters before the age of twenty-one, so that he or she will absorb these matters. A person should absorb and internalize religious values along with the practical, theoretical, intellectual and logical aspects of religion as a whole before the age of twenty-one, as this helps them to have a firm religious grounding. It is reported by Tirmidhi that the Messenger of God said, "You should teach your children how to perform daily prayers starting from the age of seven."[43] Before the age of seven, a child will imitate what you do through innate curiosity. Your duty after any action is to explain the meaning of your action, or behavior to the child. You should encourage or warn the child about the consequences of certain actions, if necessary. This means that explaining or teaching things by setting an example and by using the correct behavioral method is important when the child is young. It will be important later to explain to the child some issues in more details, according to the level of comprehension, after the child has reached a certain age. In the light of these explanations and proofs offered to the child, one can argue that children should be regarded as being mature in the eyes of God when they are reach the age of six, eight or, at the latest, ten, and should be respected. Children should be treated with great care and everything should be thought through with a Prophetic patience. The same care and patience should be displayed when teaching our children how to pray.

God's Messenger is reported to have said, "A sense of modesty is an important aspect of faith."[44] In a different Prophetic tradition he said,

---

[43] *Sunan at-Tirmidhi*, "Salat" 182.

[44] *Sahih Muslim*, "Iman" 57, 58; *Sahih al-Bukhari*, "Iman" 3; *Sunan Abu Dawud*, "Sunnah" 14; *Sunan an-Nasa'i*, "Iman" 16; *Sunan ibn Majah*, "Mukaddimah" 9.

"One who has no sense of modesty has no faith."[45] Therefore, we need to work with children when they are young, if we want them to grow up to be faithful, decent, well-mannered children who have internalized the moral values of the Qur'an and who will set a good example to others with their behavior when they are grown up.

---

[45] Ali al-Muttaqi, *al-Kanz al-Ummal*, 3/119.

Chapter Four

# RELIGIOUS EDUCATION
# OF THE CHILD

# RELIGIOUS EDUCATION
# OF THE CHILD

Marriage is a very serious affair in Islam and it must be dealt with due sensitivity. Couples planning to marry are not only future parents, but also future educators. Therefore, marriage should not be considered until a suitable age is reached for fulfilling this important mission.

Imam Jafar required his disciples to delay their marriages. And Abu Hanifa did not allow his disciple, Imam Abu Yusuf, to marry for a certain period, telling him: "First you should complete your training and education; you should learn the subjects well that you need to learn before you marry. Otherwise, your education will be incomplete. Besides, you must have a job in order to support your family in a decent way. When you meet these conditions, your life path will be clearer." This is how Abu Hanifa preached to his young disciple—a disciple who attained the rank of Sheikh al-Islam during the Abbasid dynasty.

Abu Hanifa, the great figure who was known as the architect of theoretical law, chose to act in such a way. Imam Jafar, who also taught not to rush into an early marriage, was one of the descendants of God's Messenger. What we should understand from such advice is that the institution of marriage requires much thought and care. In this respect, when we are deciding whom to marry, we must ask ourselves the following questions: "Is this person competent to educate children as a teacher would? Do they seem mature enough to share a life with another? Are they well equipped to prepare children in accordance to our path?" If the spouses-to-be are able to answer all of these questions in the affirmative, then this means that they are ready for marriage. But if they are incapable of self-control, if they cannot get along with the people around them, if they cause problems everyday, then they cannot be said to be ready for marriage and raising children. Making an effective contribution to the future of Muslims—which should be the aim of every individual—depends on the existence of ideal individuals and ideal families. Such a lofty aim can only be realized by people whose hearts are as pure as the Ka'ba, whose worth is as great as Mount Everest, and whose spirituality extends as far as the Lote Tree of the farthest limit. It is not a task to be carried out by those who rebel against the Almighty with impure thoughts and corrupt consciences. Well-bred and enlightened generations who have reached inward and outward maturity will—by the grace and help of Allah Almighty—realize this ideal. I would like to repeat what God's Messenger said to Habbab ibn Arat: "God will grant it, but what you need to do is fulfill the requirements of the causes."[46]

These lines from the venerable Alvarlı Efe[47] state beautifully what we are trying to say:

> If your tears turn to a stream
> If you cry like Ayyub did
> If your heart truly grieves,
> Will He not show any sympathy?
> If you go near His door
> Ready to offer all you have,
> And serve as He ordered,
> Will He not grant you a reward?

So, if our tears stream down and we exert ourselves in the search of new worlds to be discovered, we will receive good tidings at every resting place, we will sense the blessing of God each and every time, and we always keep walking toward Him without becoming entangled. This is the shape of our belief in the Almighty. We have absolute faith that He will prove us justified in our good intentions.

If parents want their children to exhibit certain types of behavior, it is of great importance that they practice such behavior themselves. In support of this, they must also be kind, affectionate, and tender. In this way, homes turn into institutions of education.

---

[46] *Sahih al-Bukhari*, "Manaqib" 25; "Ikrah" 1.

[47] Muhammed Lütfi Efendi (1868–1956), known also as Alvarlı Efe, was a respectable Sufi scholar and one of Fethullah Gülen's teachers.

## 1. Bringing up a Child with Multiple Abilities

If we want our children to be courageous, we should not frighten them with ideas of vampires, ghosts, giants, etc. We should raise them as strong individuals with a firm faith which will enable them to face up to any kind of difficulty.

If we really wish our children to have faith, all our attitudes and sensitivities in certain subjects, the way we go to bed and get up, the way we exert ourselves in prayer, the way we spread our affectionate wings over our children, must all reflect our faith in God and their hearts must be filled with such faith. We should always try to be the ideal for them, to avoid any kind of behavior which might make them feel contempt for us.

We should always try to maintain dignity and to remain elevated in their view, so that what we tell them will influence their hearts and they will not rebel against our wishes. In this respect, it can be said that a father who lacks seriousness can probably be the friend of his children; but he can never be their teacher, and he will fail to bring them up the way he wants.

Our homes should always reflect the atmosphere of a temple and an educational unit at the same time; in this way we can satisfy our children's spirituality, their hearts, and souls, thus we can save them from being slaves of their material desires.

## 2. Making Our Children Familiar with Mosques at an Early Age

In the Age of Happiness (the period corresponding to the lifetime of the Prophet Muhammad, peace and blessings be upon him), children were free to go to the mosque at any time they wanted, no matter what age they were. It is a pity that nowadays we think that we will violate the sanctity of a mosque by taking children along. Likewise, it is such a pity that in many mosques we see elderly people shooing children away, frightening them.

Unfortunately, these narrow-minded people think that they are preserving the dignity of the mosque by frowning on the children's actions. In fact, what they are doing merely contradicts the tradition of God's Messenger. He counseled Muslims that while standing in prayer in a mosque that the men should stand in front, then small boys, and then women and girls.

If this order of placement is followed, children will witness the pleasure and zeal of the adults at prayer; consequently, they will become more eager to practice their religion. Thus, rather than frightening them away, we should be trying to encourage them with small gifts, if possible, so that they warm towards prayer. We should make them love the mosques and their gardens, yet always strive to keep the sanctity of the mosque alive in their attitudes. When God's Messenger prayed in the mosque, he would take his granddaughter, Umamah, on his back, leaving her on the ground when he prostrated, and he would then take her on his back again before he stood up. This act is very important, as it is an example presented by God's Messenger, the ultimate guide. The glorious Prophet never used an expression or held an attitude that could be considered harsh concerning the matter of children being taken to mosques. Therefore, a beautiful corner of our neighborhood should be spared for a mosque and our homes should be places of prayer; children will see aspects of life that will remind them of God in everything that they see around them; they will look at life in pious wisdom, they will choose their path and walk that way by their free will and conscience. Let us consider the prescribed prayers. When a child is old enough to pray, the father should hold his child's hand, take his child up to the prayer rug of the mother, inspiring spiritual depth and hearty devotion to Islam. Obtaining the expected result will be a great achievement, for prayers are of essential importance in terms of turning to God.

## 3. Answering the Questions in the Child's Mind from the Very Beginning

Your children may have some questions concerning prayers and other religious matters. Introverted children are usually too shy to ask their parents such questions. However, it is of great importance that children open up and ask any questions on their minds concerning these subjects. If we leave such questions unanswered, then the questions will grow up alongside the child, and in the long run, doubts and hesitations will turn into a venomous snake that will poison their hearts.

Sometimes these doubts in the inner world of a child can become such a rapid-growing wound that one day they could cause the spiritual collapse of our child, but we may not comprehend the situation until it is too late. The child may even seem to be praying with you at the mosque, saying "There is no deity but Allah." In reality, however, such a child may have yielded to his inner conflict, and may be lost in a spiritual chaos. When we send our child to university in order that they will achieve social status and succeed to a bright future, it is inevitable that they will adopt some thoughts and attitudes that are incompatible with our religion, unless the child has had a proper spiritual background. From this point of view, the child should never be deprived of mental, emotional, and spiritual back-up that is suitable to the child's age. In the past, children used to be entrusted to nannies. While looking after the children, these nannies would educate them spiritually as well, reaching into their inner world. In fact, this kind of education should be given to them by the parents themselves. If this cannot be, then they should ensure that this responsibility is fulfilled by a capable child-minder. In this way, parents will prevent their children from going astray. A firm belief, a sound consciousness of servanthood and perfected morality can only be realized through utmost sensitivity.

## 4. Worshiping and Praying within Sight of Our Children

There should be a place and time for performing our prayers at home. We should either perform our prayers at home in congregation, if possible, or we should take our children to the mosque, holding their hands on the way. The latter option is actually more practical, especially if the mother cannot perform the prayers on certain days (during menstrual period, etc.). As she does not pray on these days, the children might think: "I guess worship and prayer are optional." That is why it would be a good idea to take our children to mosque particularly on these days. Yet, there is another way to eliminate such misunderstandings: On the days when women are not responsible for prayers, the mother may just perform ablution as usual, sit on the prayer rug, open her hands to the Almighty, and pray to Him. If she does this, she gains the merit of having performed the prayer as well as saving her children from possible misunderstandings. In Islamic reference books, this kind of behavior is also recommended. This is of essential importance in bringing up a child. When we act in this way, what the child sees around him or her will be prostrating heads, weeping eyes and hands open for praying. Your child will always be conscious of a servanthood fully recognized.

There will come a time when the *adhan* (call to prayer) is heard, and even if you do not hear the *adhan*, your child will warn you like an alarm clock, saying *"Dad/Mum, it's time to pray!"* You will thus reap the fruits of your labor.

In addition, you should spare time each day to pray to the Lord. At this time, a time previously determined, you should offer your prayers to the Almighty, invoking Him, thus practically demonstrating that the Exalted Creator can always be taken refuge in. It is better to pray aloud, openly. The Companions of God's Messenger learned the supplications he recited while he prayed. Most of these were reported by his wife Aisha, but there are also similar reports from Ali, Hasan and Husayn, may God be pleased with them.

This clearly indicates that in order to teach your children how to pray, you should make your prayers heard by your children. If you wish your children to be sensitive people who tremble when God is mentioned, you, above everyone else, should present a practical example for them.

In my life, I have witnessed such scenes that I cannot help but tremble when I recollect them. The sight of my grandmother's devotion to the Lord had a great influence on me. When she passed away I was just a small child, but I still remember how she used to tremble as my father recited verses from the Qur'an or started talking about Islam. She was so sensitive about these matters that if you enthusiastically said *"Allah,"* may His glory be exalted, near her, she would immediately turn pale, and would remain thus the whole day. Her behavior had a great influence on me. In spite of being illiterate, with a poor level of knowledge, her sincere prayers and genuine tears greatly influenced me. I have heard learned people preaching enthusiastically, but none of them have affected me the way my grandmother has. It seems to me that I owe my being a Muslim to the sincerity of my parents and my grandmother.

So, parents should be careful of their acts in the home. As mentioned above, even the slightest pouring out of your worries to the Almighty, or moaning in supplication at His door, or praying openly in full submission to the Exalted Creator will affect your child more deeply than anything else. The memory of the efforts you made to ensure your afterlife, which is your greatest concern, will be imprinted on your child's mind and he or she will always remember you praying in hopeful awe. In fact, you must pray as if you see the Almighty, as if you are always in awareness of being in His presence. The way you stand, bow, prostrate and sit during the prayers should all recall Him. Your condition before Him can be pictured like this: Imagine yourself as if you were meeting God, as if He says: *"My servant! Stand up and account for your deeds in the world!"* and thus we stand submissively and respectively, in expectation of His Mercy. Such a state of praying, in which we feel His Sublimity and fully recognize our pettiness, is a genuine stimulant to all the people in the household, including ourselves. In a *hadith* (Prophetic saying)—although we are not sure of its authenticity—God's Messenger stated: "I have such a moment with God that, at that very moment neither the angels of the highest rank nor any other creature can come close to me."[48]

So, should we have such a time, such an illuminated moment, and our children will be inspired from that moment of ours for their own prayers, when the time comes. In the future, whenever our children come up against a danger that may corrupt their faith and their worship, the memory of you praying will come to their rescue, like a guide to show them the way.

I assure you that it will work this way, since in chapter Yusuf, the Qur'an alludes to such a psychological fact. We know that the Prophet Yusuf was not a person to be tempted by a woman. However, the Qur'an states the following:

> Certainly, she was burning with desire for him; and he would have desired her had it not been that he had already seen the argument and proof of his Lord (concerning chastity and good conduct, and so was anxious only about how to escape her). (Yusuf 12:24).

Although a disputed fact, according to some of the greatest scholars who have expounded the Qur'an, the sign Yusuf saw was the image of his father Prophet Yaqub, who put his hand over his mouth and called

---

[48]  Al-Ajluni, *Kashf al-Khafa*, 2:173.

out "Yusuf!" in astonishment. This event brought Yusuf to his senses, Yusuf who was a paragon of chastity, making him exclaim: *"God forbid!"*

Your tearful eyes and sincere refuge in the Lord will play a vital role in your child's future life to help prevent a possible downfall. These will become such vivid pictures in the child's subconscious that your image will virtually be saying: *"My dear child, what are you doing!"* when they meet any kind of temptation, serving as a guide leading them away from various dangers.

## 5. Respect for the Qur'an

Reciting the Qur'an to your children and teaching them how to read it is of great importance, but there is something that is even more important. That is giving your children the sense that what is being recited is *"the Word of Allah."* Nowadays, one of the common problems we meet is that—unfortunately—the Qur'anic verses recited by some people just do not go beyond mere sound. If you can set a good example by reciting the Qur'an and do so as if you were reciting it before the Almighty Lord or beside the blessed soul of God's Messenger, then you will have conquered the hearts of those around you once again. If you let your tears stream down your cheeks while you recite the Qur'an, your child will learn much. Reciting the Qur'an flatly may lead us to becoming insensitive.

A *hadith* declares the following: "The person who recites the Qur'an most beautifully is the one who recites it in a solemn sadness." Another *hadith* states: "The Qur'an was revealed in a sad fashion."[49]

Given that the Qur'an deals with human beings, who have various worries (they surely do), we must reflect due sadness when we recite it. One of the most important points in attaining this level is to understand what the Qur'an is telling us. We must respect the Qur'an, even if we do not understand what it says, for it is the word of Allah. However, if we make some efforts to understand its meaning, then this is an indication of further respect for it. Moreover, your child will feel the teachings of the Qur'an more deeply in his heart and mind, and in this way, he will satisfy his spiritual thirst to the extent that his level of understanding allows.

---

[49] *Ibn Maja*, "Iqama" 176; "Zuhd" 19.

Those who are content with understanding only the literal meaning can be considered as having a poor sense or understanding of religion. As for those who do not have even that slight connection with the Qur'an, they are at a total loss. Learning the deeper meanings of Qur'anic verses and teaching what we have learned to our children bear the utmost significance in terms of attaining the rewards promised by the Qur'an.

As an explanation of the *hadith* mentioned above, Hafiz Munawi narrates the following event: "A little boy was about to complete learning the Qur'an by heart. He spent the nights reciting the Qur'an and performing prayers, and in the morning he went to his teacher, pale and tired. His teacher was a great scholar and a true spiritual guide. He inquired of his students about that boy. His students replied: 'O master, that student of yours keeps on reciting the Holy Qur'an until the morning light without sleeping, and in the morning he comes to your lesson.' The master did not wish his student to recite the Qur'an in this manner, so he advised the following: 'The Glorious Qur'an must be recited in the same fashion as it was revealed, my son.' And he added 'From now on, you will recite it as if you are delivering what you learned to me.' The boy left and that night, he recited the Qur'an as his master had told him. In the morning, he went to his teacher and said, 'Sir, I only managed to recite the first half of the Qur'an.' His master said: 'Alright son, tonight, I want you to recite the Qur'an as if you are reciting it before God's Messenger.'"

"This time, the student recited the Qur'an more carefully. He thought excitedly to himself: 'I am going to recite the Glorious Qur'an before the very person to whom it was revealed.' In the morning, he told his master that he was able to recite only a quarter of the Qur'an. On seeing the progress his student was making, the master elaborated the task step by step, as any good tutor would do, and he said: 'Now, this time you will recite the Holy Qur'an, imagining the moment when the blessed angel Gabriel revealed it to God's Messenger.' The next day, the student came back and told his master: 'O master, I swear by God that I only managed to recite one chapter last night.' And finally, his master said: 'My son, now recite it as if you are reciting before the Almighty Lord, Who is beyond thousands of veils. Think that God is listening to what you recite, following what He previously revealed for you.' In the morning, the student came to his master weeping: 'Master, I recited

'*Praise be to God, the Lord of the worlds,*' and I went on until '*Master of the Day of Judgment*' but I just couldn't manage to say '*Only You do we worship*'. I just worship so many things, I bow in submission before so many things that I could not dare say '*Only You do we worship*' when I imagined I was reciting it before The Lord.'"

Hafiz Munawi states that this boy did not live much longer and passed away a few days later. The wise spiritual trainer who helped him attain this level stood beside his grave, contemplating the young man in the Hereafter. Then, the boy called out from the grave: "*O master, I am alive. I have attained such a spiritual rank that I was not called to account for my deeds.*"

Reciting the Glorious Qur'an by reflecting upon the meaning of the verses, considering every single word and showing due respect to Allah's word is vital for the opening up of our hearts; these genuine feelings draw both the one who recites it and the one who listens to the recitation into the blessed climate of the Qur'an, the gates of Heaven open wide.

By narrating this event, I am not trying to say "do not recite the Qur'an unless you feel this way." On the other hand, paying due heed to what the Qur'an tells us is a necessity of being honored as His addressee. If Qur'anic verses do not effect great changes within our souls, then they cannot be expected to dominate our individual and social lives. We should be changed by the Qur'an, we should turn to Qur'anic horizons and we should keenly sense its depths; in this way will it open up its mysteries to the vision of our hearts.

Let us get back to the event we mentioned previously. That youngster did not die. He had merely returned to his Dear Lord. The excitement within his soul which was caused by the Qur'anic verses stopped his heart and he walked toward the Almighty. Surely, he would live forever. He had not been able to go beyond "*Only You do we worship,*" so he kept repeating this until the dawn. Once, another person had the same experience inside the Ka'ba. When his head touched the wall of the Ka'ba, he said: "O, Lord!" and he just stopped spellbound... He was unable to go on any further, possessed by the thought: "Are you capable of saying that? Why don't you give up hypocrisy?" Nevertheless, what that man experienced can neither be expressed, nor can such a feeling be explained to other people. This is what he felt for a few moments. Even the man himself could not later explain his feelings.

In conclusion, if we maintain a certain attitude that reflects how devoted we are to the Qur'an and if our acts indicate our inclusion in the Prophet's circle, then our environment will rapidly bloom, just like green plants after a spring shower; there will be successive revivals, and the angels will envy our life.

## a) Not Causing Our Children to Dislike Religion

In the recent past, the encouragement and instruction in points of our religion have not been properly conveyed to younger generations in Muslim countries. When we look at the situation with a pure heart and a sound mind, we will see that the underlying reason is ignorance and indifference about "meaning." Unfortunately, believers say: *"We have faith in Allah,"* but they are not fully conscious of the meaning inherent in this statement. They are unable to maintain the coordination between the outer world and their inner worlds, and they fail to comprehend religious concepts correctly. This has been a recurring error throughout history.

Even now, we cannot say that we are making good use of the opportunities granted to us by God. When our children come to us with questions concerning religion on their minds, our duty is to fill their hearts with the love of Allah and His Messenger, rather than intimidating them by obliging them to memorize some prayers, prayers which if left to time, they will learn spontaneously in the future. If we feel content with teaching our religion as if it were only a set of formalities to be learned by heart, our children may end up feeling antagonized by our religion. After just one lesson, they may refuse to learn. We do not feed a six-month-old baby with adult food.

Likewise, we should not insist that children memorize until they are of age. Hopefully, they will try to learn what they should without being told to do so. Our approach should be based on making them love, think about and internalize Islam.

Believers must be sensitive to this subject and try to make religion as enjoyable as possible. They should try to open up their children's hearts and minds to spirituality. They should love the Qur'an so much that they will be saying *"O, Almighty Allah! Grant me the ability to comprehend the religion, enable me to learn the divine purposes so that I shall be filled with Qur'anic truth"* and their life will become centered around this perspective.

## b) Continuing the Routine of Obligatory and
## Non-Obligatory Worship

Parents should perform their religious duties properly, no matter what conditions prevail, so that their children will not see any lapse in their servanthood to the Lord. God's Messenger never abandoned performing *tahajjud* (the supererogatory night prayer) and he had particular prayers which he recited when he got up in the night. He would perform a "makeup" prayer whenever he missed the recitation of these prayers, even though they were not obligatory. In this way, he clearly demonstrated that any practice of worship at home or outside is never to be abandoned.

The Companions of the Prophet were perfectly aware that once you commenced a practice of worship, you should continue in the same manner. Abdullah ibn Amr ibn As, who was one of the ascetics of the time, wished to fast everyday and keep vigil at prayer every night until dawn. Furthermore, when he married, he kept away from his wife for days. When his wife complained to God's Messenger through her father-in-law, Abdullah ibn Amr ibn As had to go to God's Messenger and he was reprimanded for neglecting his wife. That day, God's Messenger wanted him to reduce his supererogatory worshipping; yet Abdullah ibn Amr insisted on worshipping more and said: "O God's Messenger, I am capable of performing more." In the end, God's Messenger convinced him to fast every second day, to sleep for one third of the night and to keep vigil for the rest. This is reported in *Sahih al-Bukhari* and *Sahih Muslim*. Later, this blessed Companion said to another: "I wish I had agreed with what God's Messenger had told me. It is so difficult to keep up such practices at this old age. Nevertheless, I don't want to abandon the supererogatory worshipping I have been performing. I want God's Messenger to find me exactly as he left me."

Abdullah ibn Amr is a good example; one should not abandon habitual worship. God's Messenger stated that "The most meritorious kind of worship is the one that is performed steadily, even if it is of little amount."[50] If you cannot do much, stick to what you can and perform such prayers regularly, so that your child will form a good opinion of you. If you can only perform the obligatory and the *sunnah* (the Proph-

---

[50] *Sahih al-Bukhari*, "Tahajjud" 7.

et's Tradition) prayers, you should perform them thoroughly. If you have begun to perform any kind of supererogatory prayer (*tahajjud*, *awwabiyn*, *duha*, etc.), you should continue to do so. Otherwise, your child may wonder why you are neglecting them. Through keeping a steady habit of worship, the subconscious of your child will be dominated by positive views on prayer.

So far, what we have discussed appeals to those who share our way of thinking. This is the path we need to choose, if we are to bring up our children as sensitive, pious and learned Muslims. Every aim is achieved through a particular method. In order to enable our children to attain happiness in this world and in the Hereafter, our method should be to set them a practical example. All this may sound like some complicated prescription, but it is not that difficult to carry out.

## c) Respect for the Sacred Concepts

There are certain concepts that bear utmost sanctity. Belief in God is a pillar of Islamic faith. One who does not believe in God cannot be said to have an Islamic life or faith. We should keep in mind that the conquest of our children's hearts by these exalted and sacred notions is our responsibility when they come of age (usually the ages between 7 and 9 is considered an ideal time). Ensuring that a child lives with the remembrance of God's Messenger can be achieved by talking about Allah at home, every now and then. If your primary topic of conversation is the celebrities who appear on TV, then these people will naturally dominate the imagination of your child. He will tell you the names of various movie stars, sportsmen, musicians and other celebrities easily, but he will be unable to memorize even a few of the names of the Companions of our Prophet. His memory and subconscious will be occupied by useless things.

Our actions must reflect due respect for anything sacred to us. The Ka'ba for instance, is a sacred place. When you express your feelings about the Ka'ba near your child, you should be very respectful. When we step into the borders of the Ka'ba or approach Medina, our feet should touch the ground with full respect. We should even go so far as to say—as did Imam Malik—"This is not a place to go ride or walk with shoes." Whenever that great *imam* reached the borders of Medina, coming from a long distance to teach *hadith* at Masjid-i Nabawi (the Prophet's Mosque) or another mosque, he would dismount and say that this was the way one should act within that city. Naturally, any child who observes this kind of behavior will overflow with respect for the owner of Ar-Rawda[51].

The same goes for the Glorious Qur'an. The Qur'an states:

> And whoever venerates the public symbols and rituals set up by God (such as Jumu'ah and Eid Prayers, the call to the Prayer, the Sacrifice, and the rites of the Pilgrimage), surely it is because of the true piety and the God-consciousness of their hearts. (Al-Haj 22:32).

The source of the veneration of the sacred rites is piety of the heart. Piety of the heart is to be attained through the heart's recognition of God, by turning to Him in respect, by taking refuge in Him, by obeying Him and by discerning the Divine Truth. This kind of veneration is of vital importance. Mosques, for instance, will have such an exalted place in the child's mind that he will think all the roads to God start from the mosques.

When the beautiful voices of the *muezzins* call out from minarets, saying *"Allahu Akbar"* (God is the Greatest), your child should echo the words of the *adhan*, and when it is over, they should open their hands and recite the *adhan* prayer (O Allah! Lord of this perfect call and of the *salah* to be performed, grant our Prophet nearness to Haqq, reaching Heaven and beyond; and elevate him to the *Maqam al-Mahmud*—The Praised Position—which You have promised him).

In conclusion, if we nurture love for God, if we really have feelings of respect for the essentials of Islam, then we should convey these feelings to our children's hearts, show them the greatness of God, make them love Him and take His love very much to heart, so that our children will see that there is no one else to be truly loved, sought for or longed for other than the Absolute Lord. In a *hadith* which Tabarani reported to have been narrated by Abu Umama, God's Messenger stated: "Make God's servants love God, so that God will love you."[52] God can be loved only by being familiar with Him; human beings are friend-

---

[51] The place between Prophet Muhammad's tomb and the pulpit of his mosque which is called "a Garden from the Gardens of Paradise" as reported in a *hadith* (*Fath al-Bari*, 1888).

[52] Munawi, *Fayd al-Qadir*, 3:371.

ly to what is familiar and hostile to what is strange. Pagans or atheists are hostile to God because of their ignorance of Him. If such people knew him well they would love Him. In the Qur'an Allah decrees: *"I have not created the jinn and humankind but to (know and) worship Me (exclusively)."* (Adh-Dhariyat 51:56). Ibn Abbas and Mujahid interpret the expression "except to worship Me" as 'so that they become familiar with Me', which means if one is familiar with God, then one is fulfilling one's duty as a servant; if not, then one is ungrateful to one's Lord.

So, first of all we should make a child familiar with God, then the child's heart will be full of His love and they will pay due respect to Him. There must be a particular way of introducing God, a way which suited to the age of the child. Merely stating the fact that the dinner on the table comes from Him can be sufficient to make our point. At an older age, it would be wise to tell the child that the rain, which all humans, animals and plants need, pours down from the sky by the Grace of God; the showers which enliven the earth overflow from His treasures of Mercy. To an older child, we need to tell about more intricate physical facts, such as how evaporation takes place, how rain pours down in tiny drops, and explain why none of these can be the result of pure coincidence; we need to tell them that everything takes place through His bestowal. As for children of further discernment, you can tell them about God, using factual support put forward by contemporary science.

Once God's Messenger stated the following: "Love God for He grants blessings to you; love me, for I am His Messenger; and love my family for you love me."[53]

It is not difficult to make your children love God's Messenger and his Companions, so long as you find the right method. If we give them the blessed life story of the Prophet to read instead of more frivolous books, or at least provide them with Yusuf Kandahlawi's *Hayatu's-Sahaba* (Life of the Companions), a very good reference book, then they will have a chance to learn about our Prophet, his Companions and about the children of the Companions. In this way, each of these blessed people will have a high place in our children's view; they will be aching to be as cou-

---

[53] *Tabarani*, 3:46.

rageous as Hamza Abd al-Muttalib, as strong as Ali ibn Abu Taleb, as truthful as Abu Bakr as-Siddiq and as just as Umar ibn al-Khattab.

It is of utmost significance that the Qur'an, the life story of our Prophet and other books on the life of his Companions have a place of honor at home; our children's hearts will be saturated with and illuminated by our historical figures.

I would like to draw your attention to an important point here. Although using different arguments against philosophical theses and notions that threaten our faith is a logical reaction, merely dealing with just logic can damage our spiritual life and lead us to despair. After having grasped a logical explanation, your child will want to see some practical examples. Even if you construct a beautiful ladder that ascends with thousands of subjective and logical proofs for the existence and oneness of God, if you fail to give practical examples from life your child will find all these proofs too theoretical and difficult to comprehend; he might perceive the religious thought that you were trying to present as nothing more than some obscure philosophical view.

If you do not make it clear that what you are talking about really took place at a certain period in history, it may just sound like a fairy tale. This is why we have to show children that certain principles were put into practice and can be put into practice again.

Until quite recently, it has sometimes been said: "What is said about the Companions may be true, but probably this has only happened once and it is nearly impossible for such things to happen again." Such negative thoughts were like an epidemic. However, when we see the young people today who know the Exalted Creator and His Glorious Messenger and who love them deeply, then we can believe that there can again be a community whose lifestyle resembles that of the Companions. Considering the hints and glad tidings given in the Qur'an and supported by the *hadith*, we can have faith in the advent of a community described by God's Messenger as being the "*ghuraba*," the people who are regarded as strangers in their own land because of their belief and life styles who will present Islam's exalted values.

The piety in your heart, the love, and veneration you have for God, your respectful acts towards mosques and the sacred rites will seem to a child as radiant signs that invite him to God's path.

*Adhan* is a symbol of Islam and a means of concentration before the prayers. At the same time, *adhan* is an invitation from God to His servants to fulfill their duties, a reminder of His Greatness. If you manage to bring up your children with such feelings in their hearts, whenever they hear the *adhan*, they will be on the verge of tears, moved, excited and full of love for the Lord; they will tremble like a leaf. In spite of all misfortunes, this sacred duty was properly carried out by previous Muslims and—if God wills—it will be carried out again with the same effectiveness in the near future. We will teach new generations to pay due homage to the pillars of Islam, we will teach everyone to love Allah and His Messenger.

To sum up, our religious duties should be thoroughly fulfilled at home; any doubts or hesitations concerning our religion and faith in our children's minds should be eliminated as early as possible. In addition, there should be certain times of the day when we pray to the Almighty, when Divine Mercy flows in abundance, when we turn to God in supplication, expecting His Mercy; at a particular hour our hearts will overflow with sadness. In such an hour as this, the presence of God's Messenger will be felt in the home through the behavior of the master and the mistress.

The values your child will acquire in this way are so great and priceless that in his future life he will enjoy the fruits of your efforts and pray for you in gratitude.

Respecting the sacred pillars means to accept and display the greatness of values that are held dear by Islam. The love of the Most Exalted One will blossom in young hearts with *"Allahu Akbar"* during *adhan*, this love will wave like a flag in their spiritual worlds, it will possess their hearts completely, and you will be gratefully smiling in return for these divine blessings.

## 6. The Significance of Reading

One of the most important subjects in educating your child is "books and reading." Children should have a target of learning how to read and write, they should not want to be led, but rather promote themselves to the level of a guide. To know why you read is as important as reading itself.

Let us think about the following questions: "What is knowledge? What is the purpose of knowledge? Why do people read books? What is the target that we desire to reach by reading and understanding something?"

If a person learns the complex and confusing rules and principles of mathematics, but ignores their practical applications or never thinks of improving their knowledge with theories and hypotheses then they cannot be considered as having realized their goal.

Likewise, if we learn all the basic principles of medicine, but do not put this knowledge to use, not even examining a single patient, it is doubtful whether we will be able to keep up our knowledge, not to mention the fact that we have wasted our knowledge.

In short, knowledge in which we do not find anything that relates to ourselves or to someone else is, obviously, of no use to anyone.

## a) Reading and Writing

It is an accepted fact that a major priority established by the Qur'an is reading and writing. However, I would like to emphasize that just filling up your memory without trying to discern the divine purpose is not commendable. We should take a child by the hand, let their soul enjoy the Qur'an and arouse their interest in the Qur'an. Thus, in the future, that child will try to discern what God demands from us. Unfortunately, we think that we have done enough by merely telling the child to say *"Bismillah"* (in the Name of Allah). In fact, *"Bismillah"* is very important, and it consolidates faith. On the other hand, there is a matter of further importance. That is, we must teach the Divine Purposes (no matter how briefly); these are what must be taught and learned above all else. There are several glorious periods in our history. In a certain period, there were some governors, judges, and jurists who knew the Qur'an by heart in every Muslim country. However, these people did not grasp the essence of what they were studying; rather they just copied those who had preceded them, unable to put forth any fresh comments on scientific or religious matters. They lacked the ability to make sound judgments.

There came a time when these narrow-minded people, who clung to their insufficient knowledge, persisted in committing sins by keeping silent about some methods and principles that contradicted our religion. Naturally, these people failed to preserve the dignity and honor of Islam. Unfortunately, their efforts mocked our people and our religion. Their knowledge was not internalized nor did it guide their hearts. The Qur'anic verse *"He whom God guides, he is indeed rightly guided; and he whom He leads astray—they are the losers."* (Al-A'raf 7:178) is explained as follows, in a *hadith*, reported by Huzayfa bin al-Yaman to Hafiz Abu Ya'la:

> "One of the things I worry about you is that a person who reads the Qur'an so much reflects the brilliance of the Qur'an in all their behavior. Islam becomes a dress for them. They are clad with this dress until the time appointed by God comes. Then, all of a sudden—may God protect them—they take off that dress and abandon it. They approach their brothers brandishing their sword, accusing them of *shirk* (associating partners with God)." Huzayfa asked: "O God's Messenger, who is nearer to shirk; the one who is accused of *shirk* or the one who accuses of *shirk*?" God's Messenger answered: "The one who accuses of *shirk*."[54]

Even today, there are so many people with important titles who live in sheer ignorance, who neither know God nor His Messenger. The ones who fail to reflect on the thousands of verses and proofs in the universe, the ones who are indifferent to the facts and events around them are absolutely ignorant, no matter what their titles are. Since what we acknowledge as "knowledge" is the knowledge which illuminates the mental and spiritual worlds of an individual, the other types of knowledge are just burdens on our brain.

The first command of the Qur'an is *"Read in and with the Name of your Lord…"* Allah does not say "read the Qur'an"; He does not say "Read what has been revealed to you." The Qur'an itself explains the meaning of the order *"Read"* and draws attention to creation by saying: *"Read in and with the Name of your Lord, Who has created."* (Al-Alaq 96:1) Here, there is also an allusion to recognizing the signs of God on the face of creation.

*"Read, and your Lord is the All-Munificent, Who has taught (human) by the pen."* (Al-Alaq 96:3–4). As we see, reading and writing are mentioned successively. So, humans will read and write; but whatever they read, they will read with the aim of discerning their innermost faculties, the essence of the Qur'an and sensing the divine power beyond the creation and the laws of the universe. From time to time, they will look into their own physiology and anatomy; sometimes they will observe the

---

[54] Ibn Kathir, *Tafsir al-Qur'an*, 3:59.

creation. As a result, they will convey the spiritual outcome of their reflection to others, beginning with their own family.

The subsequent verses suggest what is meant by the order *"Read"* is not merely reading Qur'anic verses. By ordering us to read, the Qur'an counsels us to read divine commands, to comprehend the aim of creation and to discover the laws of the universe. Therefore, when we read, we are supposed to reflect upon the creation of human beings, the laws of the universe and the Revelation in God's name. The Qur'an raises the question "How were we created?" by mentioning creation. Right after this, the Qur'an directs our thoughts to the mystery of creation by saying that we are created from an *"alaq"* (clot), which is described as a drop of water in another verse.

God who orders us to read the book of the universe along with the Qur'an, presents human beings with such a lesson that everyone—from an ordinary person of the lowest level of discernment to the most distinguished thinker—will learn from this lesson to the extent that their capacities allow.

The Qur'an also mentions "the pen," which implies writing: *"Nun. By the Pen and what they write with it line by line."* (Al-Qalam 68:1) After the initial (*muqatta'a*) letter, God begins the *surah* (chapter) by taking an oath upon the pen, clearly indicating the emphasis He places on writing.

This pen can be the pen of the angels who keep a record of our deeds, the pen which has written down our destinies or it can be the pen you use at school, or somewhere else, it doesn't make any difference. The person who uses the pen makes the difference, and God's oath upon the pen involves everything we have mentioned.

## b) Knowledge Leads to Awe of God

In another verse, it is stated that: *"Of all His servants, only those possessed of true knowledge stand in awe of God."* (Fatir 35:28). Indeed, only the learned are truly respectful of God, since the sense of respect in divinity depends on knowledge. The ones who do not know God and who are ignorant of the mystery of divinity obviously lack due respect and awe.

Starting off from this point of view, if we want to raise our children well, one of the most important things to do is to instill in the child a firm belief. They should also be informed, as much as possible, about the proofs of the Almighty Lord's existence. Sometimes, such proofs might eliminate your doubts, but they can be difficult to understand for a child. If this is the case, then other approaches should be tried.

Another important point is to conquer their hearts with love for the Prophet. In order to realize this, we need to tell them about his life.

### c) Elimination of Doubts

Nowadays, we come up against many questions like "Who has created the universe?" or—God forbid—"Who has created God?" The commonness of such questions indicates that children have not been given a satisfactory explanation concerning God. The underlying reason behind the question "Why did the Prophet have more than one wife?" is just the same. The child who asks this question does not have proper information concerning God's Messenger.

Likewise, some people make comments like: "God's Messenger was a very intelligent man. The changes he made were the results of his intelligence." Obviously, these people lack religious education and they are not aware of the real meaning of "Prophethood".

Moreover, if misinformation arises from society, this just makes matters worse. We should feed the spiritual world of our child with healthy ideas, so that in the future they will have a firm belief. If what you tell a child is appropriate for the age of that child, then it will be convincing for them. In this way, you will have eliminated some possible doubts that may have arisen in their minds.

Once the Zoroastrians (fire-worshippers) asked Abu Hanifa some questions, and demanded satisfactory answers. They told Abu Hanifa that they did not believe in God, at a period when both scientific progress and Islamic thought were on the rise. There were many Zoroastrians in Kufah, the city where Abu Hanifa lived.

Abu Hanifa explained everything to them in a very simple way: "If you see a boat heading with ease for the shore in a rough sea, expertly steered and keeping a steady course, in spite of the waves, will you doubt that there is somebody on board, steering it with perfect skill?" They replied in a chorus: "No, we wouldn't!" Then the great *imam* asked: "So, these stars, this vast universe, the earth steer easily through the sea on a steady course; how can you think that all this happens on its own?" On hearing this, the Zoroastrians said: *"La ilaha illa'llah, Muhammadu'r-Rasulullah."* (There is no deity but Allah, and Muhammad is His Messenger).

Here, what he did was to make the explanation suit the level of the people he was addressing. For some, this may be too simplistic, while for others it may be sufficient. No matter how logical such an explanation is, after a certain age is reached, it will no longer suffice. When the time comes, we need to make the argument with ideas that require deeper thought. We can give various examples using the universe, human biology, etc. The human body, its inner mechanisms, its cells, systems, anatomy, and physiology are all created to an amazing degree of perfection. In my opinion, introducing these examples within a scientific framework will help us to achieve the desired effect. We can also talk about the various features of air, water, light, vitamins, proteins, carbohydrates, or microorganisms. Actually, only the presentation will differ; it is merely the continuation of the same lesson. The way Bediüzzaman Said Nursi[55] spoke of God is a very good example of what we have said:

> Every village must have its headman. Every needle must have its manufacturer and craftsman. And, as you know, every letter must be written by someone. How then, can it be that so extremely well-ordered a land should have no ruler?[56]

Asking how the universe, so vast and magnificent, can be left unattended and asking how things can happen on their own is a good method to get a child to start thinking. If we go through the available publications on this subject, we can obtain plenty of material. All we need to do is to pick out the right subjects for the young people we are addressing.

## 7. Speaking about the Age of Happiness and God's Messenger

We must be very sensitive about introducing God's Messenger. The fact that some people dislike the Messenger of God nowadays can be attributed to the fact that they were not informed about him during their childhood. The ones who knew him well admire and adore him.

---

[55] Bediüzzaman Said Nursi (1877–1960) is one of the greatest Muslim thinkers and scholars of the 20th century. He wrote about the truths and essentials of the Islamic faith, the meaning and importance of worship, morality, and the meaning of existence, and he was very original in his approach. *Sözler* (The Words), *Mektubat* (The Letters), *Lem'alar* (The Gleams), and *Şualar* (The Rays) are among his most famous works.

[56] Nursi, Said. *The Words*. New Jersey: The Light. 2010, p. 68.

Throughout the centuries, masses of people, fascinated by his charm, have followed him, and no man in the world history has been thus respected. However, we can not expect our children to love God's Messenger without telling them about him. At a certain time period, there was a fortunate group of people who had the honor of seeing and being with him. Another fortunate group saw the ones who saw him and tried to see him through the eyes of the preceding generation. This is summed up in the *hadith*: "The best among you (are) the people (who belong to) my age. Then those next to them ..."[57]

God's Messenger came at a very dark time; at that time there were heartless people who buried their daughters alive, almost everyone drank alcohol and there was a very weak moral code. Such a blessed person, one who accomplished an incredible social reform, all of his achievements and his community are absolutely peerless throughout all of history.

Some revolutions took place in Ancient Greece, Rome and in other countries also. However, none of these offered much in terms of human values. These revolutions brought new problems and in some places there was a return to the past. We can even say that in certain periods, what was left behind by revolutions was nothing but blood and tears.

A real revolution is one which effects positive changes within the hearts, the souls, the social and spiritual life, the feelings, and thoughts of the people; one which frees them from the grasp of the carnal self and elevates them to the top of humanity, resulting in a chain of pure generations. This is what God's Messenger, the greatest expert on social life, achieved as a Prophet, thanks to his excellent ability at dealing with social matters. Unfortunately, we have neglected to learn about him and to convey any knowledge about him to our children, although he set an ideal example in every aspect of life.

Here is another point from Bediüzzaman Said Nursi: "... a small habit like smoking in a small community can be removed permanently only by a powerful ruler and with great effort."[58] To paraphrase this: If ten people try to persuade a heavy smoker to give up smoking, telling him how it causes cancer in a most convincing manner, they will still not

---

[57] *Sahih Muslim*, "Fada'il al-Sahaba" 210.
[58] Nursi. *Ibid*. p. 250.

be able to make him give up smoking. On the other hand, God's Messenger abolished all the evil habits of the people around him, something which seemed impossible at the time, replacing these with the most exalted human values.

The incredible obedience to the prohibition of alcohol was a remarkable fact. Imagine an alcoholic community, where alcohol is a part of life. As soon as they heard the order "alcohol is prohibited," they smashed the glass in their hand, never to drink again. Academics have failed to explain why this reform was so effective. Thus, what we need to do is to learn about this blessed person who had the greatest virtue and to speak about what we know of him to others, so that his love will conquer their hearts. When we achieve this, our children will speak about him, think about him and they will sense him. As a result, we will have direct back up in our efforts from God's Messenger. May the Almighty consolidate our faith through this blessed person!

Telling our children about God's Messenger and all the events he foretold will refresh their trust in him. In his *hadith*s, he foretold many events that would happen in the future, including their causes and their results, stretching from his time until the end of the world, and warned us about these events.

He foretold several events, such as the Mongolian invasion, the occupation of Syria, the tremendous increase in the value and importance of the river Euphrates, petroleum being found in Taleqan, the spread of corrupt morality and so on. It is virtually impossible to deny his Prophethood when one is aware of all these facts. It is our responsibility to let others know that God's Messenger revealed the knowledge of both the past and the future, despite the fact that he had never received any education, except that given by God.

He stated facts concerning medicine that would later prove to be true, even though at that time it was impossible for him to know such facts from the basic level of scientific knowledge of those times. Therefore, God taught him and he revealed what he had been taught, clearly indicating that he was truly God's Messenger. If we were to prepare a serious study concerning his deeds, volumes of books would not suffice. We have briefly mentioned some facts.

## 8. Introducing the Qur'an

Making younger generations love the Qur'an is of great importance when trying to raise their religious consciousness. Merely saying "the Qur'an is sacred" is too superficial a statement to describe the Qur'an, and to introduce it to a child. Such an attitude might seem to be appropriate at times, but it is sure to fall short in the long run; it is even harmful in that it leads to a future prejudice against religious teaching. From this point of view, we should tell and convince the child that the Qur'an is the latest and indisputable revelation from God, with decisive judgments pointing to the farthest limits of science and technology.

In fact, the Qur'an is a wonderful book which confirms all the latest scientific findings concerning the universe, creation, and existence. It even gives concise data about such subjects. We can say that it explains everything from the micro to the macro scale in terms of servanthood. The following verse confirms this point:

> With Him are the keys to the Unseen; none knows them but He. And He knows whatever is on land and in the sea; and not a leaf falls but He knows it; and neither is there a grain in the dark layers of earth, nor anything green or dry, but is (recorded) in a Manifest Book. (Al-An'am 6:59).

## 9. Teaching about the Resurrection

Our next step should be to talk about the resurrection. The child should believe in their hearts that as soon as this life ends, a new life, an everlasting afterlife, will begin. Science, wisdom, and reality point out that God created this universe and that He maintains it. He is the One Who demonstrates and fixes "time." The Qur'an alludes to this fact by the following verse: *"Say: 'Go about on the earth and see how God originated creation. Then God will bring forth the other (second) creation (in the form of the Hereafter). Surely God has full power over everything.'"* (Al-Ankabut 29:20).

Therefore, we should investigate the laws of the universe; examine everything step by step; we should see and reflect on how life began on earth, how this universe came into existence out of nothing, how human beings appeared, how various forms of life were created as different species, and how perfection was completed with human beings.

God, Who created the universe from nothing, will certainly resurrect us. Is the One Who has established this order not able to establish another? Is the One Who created this earth so splendidly not able to create another? Can He not call this world as 'worldly life', and the other one as the Hereafter? Can the One Who brought us to this world not take us to an eternal abode? Such explanations are at a suitable level for the comprehension of our children.

We can see that the skies and the earth have been created perfectly with our eyes. Like a fish swimming in the sea, or a bird soaring in the sky, those immense systems, those nebulas float by so smoothly in an enrapturing harmony through the universe, that no disorder or randomness can be seen by one who looks with eyes of wisdom. Moreover, this harmony is explicit even to the simplest mind. The Glorious Qur'an highlights all of these and points to the special significance of the creation of humans, apart from the creation of the heavens and the earth.

> God is He Who has created the heavens and the earth and what is between them in six days, then established Himself on the Supreme Throne. You have, apart from Him, no guardian (to whom you might refer the ultimate meaning and outcome of your affairs), nor any intermediary (who, without His leave, can cause anything of use to reach you). Will you not reflect and be mindful? (As-Sajdah 32:4).

> He Who makes excellent everything that He creates; and He originated the creation of humankind from clay. (As-Sajdah 32:7).

The Glorious Qur'an says God created and ordered these magnificent systems. He will create a different universe after they have been demolished. These are undeniable facts. There are a lot of unique and crystal clear statements on this subject contained in the Qur'an.

In the following verse, the Qur'an addresses those who deny resurrection:

> Say: "He Who produced them in the first instance will give them life. He has full knowledge of every (form and mode and possibility of) creation (and of everything He has created, He knows every detail in every dimension of time and space)." (Ya-Sin 36:79).

Another verse decrees:

Look, then, at the imprints of God's Mercy—how He revives the dead earth after its death: certainly then it is He Who will revive the dead (in a similar way). He has full power over everything. (Ar-Rum 30:50).

The Glorious Qur'an's articulate style, free from redundancy, will explain what needs to be told to people of every age very clearly. The Archangels and destiny are also among subjects that need to be regarded sensitively. We must make it very clear to the younger generation in different ways that everything has a program, a project, and a plan; thus so must the universe. This program called "destiny" is within divine knowledge and it includes everything that has not come into existence yet.

In conclusion, we will have shown our children the *Sirat al-Mustaqim* (the Straight Path) only after having taught all these things to them; we will have said *"Guide us to the Straight Path"* (Al-Fatiha 1:6), both in words and actions. *Insha'Allah*, we will reap the benefit of our efforts and of our practical prayer by the Grace of the Almighty Lord. By teaching our children everything from the essentials of faith to the pillars of Islam, we should direct them to the Almighty, and in this way, we will save them from mental and spiritual death.

If children grow up in a pure atmosphere, if God wills, their spirituality will not be shaken by any evil they face and they will always be obedient servants of God.

Chapter Five

---

DIMENSIONS OF EDUCATION

# DIMENSIONS OF EDUCATION

In the previous chapters, we explored the themes of teaching children according to their age level, so that what they learn is suitable to their level of understanding, and we touched upon issues that parents, teachers and educators should put importance in.

It would be good to remember here, once again, that those who are not careful about nurturing their children and who do not provide for their physical, intellectual and spiritual needs at every stage of their lives because they are caught up in worldly concerns, such as their career, social environment and academic progress, should not feel dismayed when they see that their child has grown into a person that is more like a ravenous wolf.

## 1. Good Deeds Should Be Introduced by Exemplary Righteous People

The issue of teaching good deeds with the examples of righteous people concerns teachers and educators rather than parents. Below we express our views concerning how we should behave when trying to teach good deeds through the example of righteous people.

Undoubtedly children and young people should learn what good deeds are. However, teaching and instruction will consist of pure theoretical knowledge and therefore, theoretical input should be supported by teaching about the exemplary lives of righteous people; it is important that good deeds should be remembered along with their heroes. People who are well known for their good deeds and their carrying out of daily prayers should be introduced to the minds of children at an early stage, allowing children to become aware that they are on an important path, a path that respected people have previously trodden on; the children will then enjoy walking along this bright path. If we are able to pass judgment on a person who performs their daily prayers and who

fasts many days of the year, despite it being hot or cold, by merely looking at the external appearance of this person, then a child, upon reaching
a certain age, should believe that this person is virtuous before God.
Eventually, whatever children do for their religion and faith is performed
according to the meaning and spirit of their belief and can never be shak-
en by any winds.

The Messenger of God is reported to have said: *"In this age hypocrites
are trying to hide their conduct from you, they are ashamed and they are hiding their state of affairs. A day will come when Muslims will also similarly hide
(their beliefs and deeds)."*[59]

Children should be informed about this disease that appears in different periods of our life. They should be taught how to overcome this
disease during their childhood and they should be prevented from stum-
bling at later stages in their lives. They should also be told that religion
is a means of honor and pride; they should be imbued with a spiritual
tendency that embraces the commands of God with a heartfelt sincerity.

Here I would like to give a true example of such a case. A female
student, a daughter of parents who had planned her education very carefully and who had followed it closely, one day started to influence her
teacher. Although she preserved her respect for her teacher, this child
was very troubled and disturbed because atheism was wearing her teacher down spiritually. One day, the girl all of a sudden started crying at the
back of the classroom; the religious truths that were nestling deep in her
heart caused her so much concern for her teacher that she could not bear
it. Then this loving teacher came up to her and asked, "Why are you crying?" She replied, "I am crying for you," and then continued, "I am sad
because God will punish you for not believing." The teacher was speech-
less and went away. After a few days she came back to the classroom,
coming up to her student, her face reflecting the beauties of belief; these
two believers were then able to share their joy.

Along with belief (faith), a sense of honor had been instilled in this
child. Honor is an attribute pertaining to God. Yet, it is a religious fact
that God will make those who fulfill their religious duties and live
according to religious principles honorable, while making those who

---

[59] At-Tabarani, *Musnad ash-Shamiyyin* 1/148.

abandon these principles contemptible. Children should have confidence, not doubt, in their feelings, thoughts and in the path that they are following, in order not to develop feelings of inferiority and to be drawn away from the true path by atheist movements. Moreover, they should perceive the performance of prayers and fasting as a superior action, thus performing their daily prayers without hesitation, showing that they only bow down before God.

Regarding the things we will or will not do in our lifetime, the Qur'an puts forward what God requires for us when embarking on the path followed by martyrs, the righteous and faithful people, in verses such as *"You alone do We worship, and from You alone do we seek help. Guide us to the Straight Path"* (Al-Fatiha 1:5–6) which we recite almost forty times a days. In the following verse, on the other hand, which reads *"The Path of those whom You have favored, not of those who have incurred (Your) wrath (punishment and condemnation), nor of those who are astray"* (Al-Fatiha 1:7), the Qur'an draws our attention to the fact that negative things will appear before us, and points out that we should take a stand against disbelief and heresy, while voicing our desire for Paradise and the path of grace.

This is the way that we should go when educating those who are under our care. We should adopt methods that will instill beautiful things in their hearts; things with which God will be pleased, while also helping to develop a reaction in their hearts and minds against the things that God disapproves of. In fact, it is our duty to nurture children in such a way. Those who do not recognize God and do not accept Him as the only ruler in their lives will be held responsible for this. For those who do not recognize the duties embedded in human nature, those who do not grasp the wisdom of creation, who have no idea why they came to this world cannot sense the relationship between cause and effect in the universe. Moreover, those who have no belief in or understanding of God, Who makes us feel His existence, cannot reach salvation, either in this world or in the Hereafter. God will grant salvation to believers or to those who maintain a relationship with the same, as expressed in the following verse:

> And do not incline towards those who do wrong (against God, by associating partners with Him or transgressing against His commands, or against people, by violating their rights), or the Fire will touch you. For

you have no guardians and true friends apart from God; (but if you should
incline towards those who do wrong,) you will not be helped (by Him).
(Hud 11:113)

## 2. Utilizing Positive Sciences in Religious Education

At the same time as children are learning about physics, chemistry, and
other positive sciences, it is necessary to teach them "the principles and
realities of Islam" at the same intellectual level as the sciences. In contrast
to a person who is a materialist and considers positivism as the basis of the
explanation for everything, a believer should utilize such material in the
context of understanding and explaining God, the Hereafter, the Qur'an,
and faith (belief). Believers should be able to grow roses in the same swamp
where historical materialists have become bogged down and they should
value things (creatures) and events as signs of the existence of God.

Children learn positive sciences as part of their education, starting in
primary school and continuing through high school and university. During this process children will inevitably be corrupted if they do not
receive religious education on the same scale within the family or immediate environment. If we do not follow what our children are learning in
school or with their friends and do not intervene against any mistaken
views introduced to them in time, then whatever they learn may lead to
blasphemy or disbelief. In fact, sciences are outspoken evidence of the
existence of God.

Children may experience serious intellectual crises at later stages if
their education is not supported by a positive analysis of reason, logic,
and the sciences instead of merely learning philosophy and possibly drift-
ing into doubt and suspicion. Therefore, children's learning should be
supported by rational, logical, and literary proofs in scale with their
learning and education.

Materialists attribute the order in the universe to nature and engage
in demagogic debates with some philosophic theories. In opposition to
this indoctrination we should explain to the child that the order in the
universe and "the laws of nature" that we can observe are under the control of God, i.e. these are His laws. Only by instilling such information
in his/her mind can we circumvent doubts and misgivings that may be
caused by various theories.

We should furnish the child's mind with sound knowledge to protect against all corrupted information and twisted views, helping the child to avoid confusion. In essence, everything is bound to knowledge. Ignorance is the major enemy of religion and of the faithful. Therefore, believers must raise a generation who are loyal to their country, nation, and roots, who are receptive to their religion, value system, sciences, learning and who can protect their own history and geography against the efforts of the people who are trying to corrupt children with various deceptions.

## 3. Preparing a Decent Environment

Now we would like to touch upon the issue of preparing a decent environment for children. In the modern world, people attach importance to nursery schools, child-care centers, and social institutions located near schools or in other suitable places. The aim here is to ensure a healthy, sound, and stable physical world and the material well-being of the child, as well as ensuring a good education without causing too much trouble to the family. All of these policies are very well-planned and their possible benefits and cost are all calculated beforehand. However, just as children need a physical environment, they also need an atmosphere where they can develop and lead their spiritual life, where they can become aware of their humane dimensions and establish a spiritual communication with their God. The provision of this spiritual dimension should also be taken into account when talking about preparing an "environment for the child." Now, we will try to explain what should be done in relation to these issues.

### a) Selection of Friends

It is very important to provide your children with the opportunity to make friends in a peer group that respects religion and spiritual values. Parents should not only confine themselves to enabling children to choose friends, but also actively follow the process of making friends. The child should be constantly observed, but not in a controlling or directional manner, rather with an aim to guide them on the path of becoming individuals who respect their religious and cultural values. Children are our most precious treasures; they should not be entrusted to just anyone. Human beings do not entrust their most valuable possessions with strangers, let alone their children. Imagine a stranger comes up to you and says, "There are a lot of pickpockets around. Your wallet is not safe, why don't you give it to me so that I can protect it for you." Would you trust that person? Of course not! You do not entrust your bag or your wallet to a stranger. Then, how can you entrust your children to someone you do not know, leaving the evaluation of their progress to a total stranger?

Eventually it is, once again, a parental responsibility to guide the child to make the right friends. As the great poet Sadi Shirazi wrote in his famous book *Gulistan* (The Rose Garden), a wicked friend is worse than a black snake or a cobra. Once they have possession of you, they either bite you or occupy you with the wrong things. A good friend is better than an angel. When you are in an angel's company, you travel through the horizons of the angels.

The Messenger of God is reported to have said, "A human being is with the one whom he or she loves."[60] Therefore, it is very important for parents to help their children find good friends. The friendship environment should never be neglected in the development of the child's emotional and mental capabilities. If children make harmful friends, they should immediately be removed from this environment and be sent to a different, safe place. If children are surrounded by bad friends in their neighborhood, then you must find a way of isolating them from such friends. If you cannot isolate them from bad friends, then you should take them from their school and send them to a different town. However, you have to ensure that the first friends that the child will make there are decent and virtuous.

No matter where children are, when they enter a social environment they should be able to find a spiritual atmosphere and to socialize with others, discussing elevated thoughts and the communication of such. A child's leaving the home will not only sadden the parents, making them long for their child, but it will at the same time lead them to greater expenditure to meet the child's needs. But parents must always live in the fear and worry of the day on which God will judge them and their children, and therefore they should work hard to be ideal parents in both

---

[60] *Sahih al-Bukhari*, "Adab" 96; *Sahih Muslim*, "Birr" 165.

the present and the future. It is fine for children to go to their friends' houses from time to time to study. But they still should be watched closely here, too.

Children should be able to visit their friends' houses, but God should be remembered in every corner of this house. When the call for prayer is heard, the members of this family should be ones who come together and perform their prayers in a congregation. If children go to study in such a house, then no obstacles should be put in their way, on the contrary, they should be encouraged to do so. But, if the house that our children go to is a place where sinful acts are committed and selfish desires are indulged, then this means you have already lost your children.

### b) Enabling Your Children to Taste a Sincere Religious Life and Keeping Them away from Hypocrisy

You should take your children to the mosque and congregational prayers. Additionally, you should take them to places where *Mawlid*[61] ceremonies are held and where they are recited. By doing this, you expose the children to different aspects of religious life. As a requirement of children's innate nature, they have a fondness of participating in such things and feel satisfied when so doing; this is a good means to forestall them searching in other areas for satisfaction. Even the music they listen to should instill their religion and spiritual values and develop their sacred feelings, preparing the way for the development of a sense of God.

I should point out here that, if, on the other hand, a child senses insincerity in these ceremonies and feels that the utterances and hymns do not have a deep influence on people, and if such insincerity shakes the foundations of a child's religious feelings, then it would be better to keep the child away from such places. Religious hymns and *Mawlid*s should be the means of the spiritual purification of the conscience. However, if there are no tears in the eyes of those chanting or reciting when they say "Whenever I remember you (God), my tears flood," then these people are being insincere before God. When a child hears such a great lie, he or she might interpret it as disrespect to his or her own feelings.

---

[61] A eulogy recited to celebrate the birth of the Messenger of God.

I remember that, as a child, when I had to write an Arabic sentence meaning, "O my God, I shiver whenever I remember you," I trembled and had to put down my pen. I still have the notebook that this writing is in as a memento. I felt ashamed because I asked myself how could I say "O my God, I shiver" when I was not trembling? When a child sees an insincere person, one who prays "O our God! We come to you crying," but sees no tears in their eyes, this may cause various questions to arise in their minds.

As you have noticed, we consider the *Mawlid* and the recitation of hymns as a religious ceremony that is an important factor contributing to the development of a child's spiritual life, yet at the same time, we feel that if such ceremonies may lead a child to lying, hypocrisy and pomposity, then it is necessary, according to religion, reason and logic, to keep the child away from such ceremonies. Children should be kept away from hypocrisy to the same extent that they should be kept away from disbelief. They should search for sincerity in religion. You should enable them to listen to those who sing what they feel deep in their hearts, not to those who chant pleasant ideas in which they do not believe.

This attitude is a requirement of our religious understanding, and we see the same issues in the lives of the Companions of the Messenger of God. In fact, this is the attitude and understanding of God's Messenger himself, and therefore one cannot imagine any other attitude being suitable for his Companions. When we accept this principle, it also means that we accept a guideline that has been accepted as a principle by religion. On the contrary, if we remain within the confines of our mistaken view, then we have prepared the ground for leading our family and children to confusion. Therefore, I recommend that you introduce your children to serious thinkers who can express the importance of religion and its grandeur, rather than taking children into the circles of hypocrites where they will listen to insincere singers. If we are thinking of protecting the future generation, then we have to keep them well away from the hypocrites.

### c) Selection of Individuals with Whom a Child Can Establish a Healthy Relation

In previous chapters, we elaborated on issues and conditions pertaining to the healthy development of a family. In fact, children who have been looked after, protected and well nurtured are protected from the negative effects of their social environment to a large extent. However, a close observation of the effect of their environment on them is still important. We should protect our children in such a way that they should not be sent even to buy books or pencils in shops where they can hear bad words or be exposed to deprecating influences. This means that they should not enter bookshops where harmful books are on display. Wherever they go, their spiritual world should never be tainted, even to the smallest degree; rather they should be able to see the pure signs of God's religion and exemplary indications of the same. I should remind you, once again, that even the shops where they will purchase such simple things as pencils should be selected by the children's parents or guardians in order to prevent others from tripping the children up.

If a child goes to a tailor for a suit, he should see his own world and hear sounds from his world. Moreover, there should be discussions on religion, religious values, the future, and progress of his country as long as he stays there and these should reflect elements of our thoughts on spiritual world of the visitors while the tailor sews the suite. The feelings and language of the tailor should express the truth; he should explore our world of thought (philosophy) several times while he prepares the suit.

Exercising such a degree of sensitivity should not be interpreted as isolating children from others. On the contrary, it should be seen as being sensitive to their developing in a positive direction. Let us look at this issue in more detail. We should take our child to a hairdresser who starts cutting his or her hair in the Name of God (by reciting *Bismillah*). He should mention the name of God when turning on the tap, when cutting the hair and when walking around. If we cannot find such a hairdresser, as it is difficult to be perfect in all aspects of our life, we will see the impact of this deficit on our children.

I would like to take this opportunity to focus on a particular point. Accepting an invitation and attending its call is seen to be a religious duty. The Messenger of God is reported to have said, "If someone invites you to a wedding or engagement ceremony, you should attend it."[62] It is obvious that one cannot oppose this order, which comes directly from

---

[62] *Sahih Muslim*, "Nikah" 98, 101; *Sunan ibn Majah*, "Nikah" 25.

God's Messenger. Facing such an order, every believer should say *"I obey
with submission"* and comply with it. However, turning down an invitation to a wedding ceremony where sinful and prohibited evil acts are to
be performed and where transgressions occur is also a reflection of a religious attitude. Children should not be taken to places that will corrupt
their thoughts or confuse them by what they see.

### d) Selecting Television Programs for Children

A Muslim who has a television set in his house should carefully select the
programs which the children are allowed to watch. It would be wrong to
say that television commits sins and does wrong things. However, it is necessary for the sake of a sound education to choose the television programs
to be watched. As a matter of fact, governments have also approached this
issue in the same way and have taken several precautions pertaining to the
protection of children. They have introduced a number of sanctions because
they also thought that some programs, political broadcasting, and various
films may be harmful to children. In fact, some programs shake the moral
and religious foundations of young people, darken their spiritual world,
and encourage them towards transgression. If a television channel is being
watched in your house, even though it conflicts with your moral values, it
is inevitable that the morals of the members of your family, including your
children, will be corrupted from within.

Such words should not be interpreted as if we are opposed to science, progress, technology, and learning. We are in favor of using and
developing technology for the well being and happiness of humanity. We
have to benefit from such blessings of God in the areas of thought, culture, industry, health, and medicine. This is not a reactionary approach.
It would be reactionary to keep silent in the face of the evil, immoral,
and corrupt broadcasting that is shown on some television channels.

### e) Raising Children with Qur'anic Training

Protecting children's hearts, minds, hearing, sight, and the other senses
from becoming accustomed to transgressions, while enabling them to
grow up in a decent environment and providing a religious atmosphere
in which they will feel at home, even when outside the house, are very
important parental responsibilities. It is also the duty of the parents, the

instructors, and educators to ensure the conformity of the external social environment with the domestic home environment.

As a matter of fact, in a period when power is used as means of oppression and the truth is being violated, it is extremely important to remain on the straight path in terms of feelings and thoughts and to preserve the honor of being human. Therefore, I believe that nurturing a generation with Qur'anic principles in education and training, enabling them to develop a Qur'anic moral value system, educating them to be loyal followers of God, and raising their physical, mental and spiritual capabilities to a level of unwavering resistance against formidable corruptive factors are among the most crucial steps in preserving our spiritual existence. One sees that the establishment of an ideal society, both in the world of the conscience and senses, and in the real world is made possible only with the Qur'an.

One can argue that the perfect Muslim society, a society enlightening a period of more than one thousand years in which it was represented by responsible people, emerged with the guidance of the Qur'an. The emergence of the Muslim society that changed the course of history is the most amazing event in human history. This perfect society and its members did not confuse their minds with other thoughts or philosophical trends; instead they achieved their progress and ideal structure through utilizing the clear source of the Qur'anic fountain.

God's Messenger's manners and morality represented those of the Qur'an. Those who followed him were living the moral values of the Qur'an found in his personality and nurturing the same in themselves from his example. Those who cannot demonstrate such perfection, although they appear to have a connection with the Qur'an, fail to grasp a deeper understanding of it. They can have only a superficial understanding of the Qur'an.

Understanding the Qur'an and its revival depends on deepening one's grasp of its core messages. Those who deal with its text may only acquire merit in God's sight—only God can know this—but they are never susceptible to good deeds. The real issue in the context of our relation with the Qur'an is to feel it with all the dimensions of our self, approaching it with our hearts, our minds, our consciousness, and our comprehension. We can feel and hear God's address and message through such an approach and in such a state of mind, and we can then experience a sudden revival. We can reach different depths in every word and in every sentence of a verse and reach a horizon where we witness maps of our spirits alongside maps of the heavens.

In my view, a new generation can only be formed in an atmosphere that is the same as the one described above; in the meantime a process of the formation of a "righteous circle" will begin. The Qur'an pours its secrets into our hearts, thus as much as we ascend from knowledge (science) to faith and from faith to wisdom with this richness, we also attain an inner profundity as a result of the differentiation in the levels of becoming His addressee. We then attain such profoundness that we are able to comprehend the immensity of God's words in a distinct way. Primarily, the action-oriented and practical-axis based discipleship of the Qur'an is the only means to unraveling the message of the Qur'an. On the contrary, if our link with the Qur'an and our respect for it remain just superficial formalism, then we will feel distanced even though we are not far away. As long as human beings are deprived of the Qur'anic message and its richness, which gives meaning to life, then they will be regarded as unlucky or destitute. The core of the problem regarding the relationship with the Qur'an is about activating the whole human system that goes beyond knowledge. It is essential to execute whatever is learned from the Qur'an, according to the conditions, circumstances, and atmosphere that one finds oneself in, by turning the acquired knowledge into a driving force. If this can be achieved, then human beings will find their place on the right track, one that is in accordance with the purpose of their creation and they will be able to avoid a disreputable extinction.

## 4. Upholding Sensitivity in Nurturing

Explaining a truth and installing a thought are one thing, while sustaining them is completely another. There have been numerous examples of ideals carefully executed and institutionalized. Although nothing is lacking in their foundations and in their day-to-day operations, neither has there been any progress, as no real attention has been paid to their development. Moreover some of these ideals and institutions are doomed to failure and have thus collapsed right at the time of their birth, due to bad management.

As a matter of fact, the construction of something is very important. However, ensuring the further development and continuation of whatever has been built is more important. The first Muslims were exceptionally careful to transmit all of the dynamics that keep a society alive in the community. They were also very cautious about the preservation of these dynamics and therefore they did not allow the emergence of logical, mental, or emotional vacuums. They made no mistake about putting into practice what they believed. Here of course I am not referring to individual mistakes. I am referring to the fundamentals of a healthy society and those necessary for its survival. At a later period, some people, who had no grasp of the core of the matter and who approached Islamic issues from a single aspect only, radically destroyed what had been accomplished, and we have been unable to develop the historical legacy we inherited. In fact, we have impoverished this heritage.

## a) Not to Become a Successor in Evil

There are a number of verses in the Qur'an which narrate the lives of the Prophets. These verses recommend the following: *"And make mention of Abraham in the Book"* (Maryam 19:41); *"And mention Moses in the Book"* (Maryam 19:51); *"Also make mention of Ishmael in the Book."* (Maryam 19:54). The Qur'an recounts characteristics of these distinguished people and explains the epochs they opened in chapter Maryam. Then the Qur'an reminds us what happened later:

> "Then, there succeeded them generations who neglected and wasted the Prayer and followed (their) lusts (abandoning the service of God's cause)." (Maryam 19:59).

Prophets Noah, Adam, Moses, Jesus or Prophet Muhammad, peace be upon all of them, may preside at the beginning of an undertaking. If their successors become bad followers, i.e. if they turn against them, or if they waste their prayers, that is if they do not miss out their prayers altogether, but rather are regarded as not having performed their prayers properly then they cannot benefit from the wisdom and experience of the great people. If the followers of these great Prophets ignore their closeness to God, opting for distance, if they indulge their sexual desires, if they practice their religion according to their own personal wishes, then these people will not be deserving heirs to the great project entrusted to them.

We have come face to face with loss, at exactly the same point where our predecessors also became lost. To follow Islam, yet ignore the daily payers because they are too much trouble, to be a Muslim, yet not fast because it is physically too difficult, and to perceive this religion as having no limits, allowing complete indulgence in physical desires all constitute bankrupt thought; this is the malady that has corrupted our age.

In fact, a believer is a representative of faith and confidence as well as a representative of submission to God in all of his or her states. As one believes in God, one stands obedient before Him and fears His prohibitions.

### b) The Importance of Performing the Daily Prayers

The Messenger of God is reported to have said: "Those who perform our prayers, who turn to our *qiblah*[63] and who eat our food are from our community."[64] Now let us think of the reverse of this statement. From which community do those come who never prostrate in prayers, who are disrespectful of others, who cause anarchy, who bear hostility towards law and order, who fight against state authority, and who try to place anarchy in the country? No matter from which community you consider such people, they have no place within God's Messenger's circle of blessed spirituality.

As a matter of fact, performing prayers is very important and therefore we should be conscious and vigilant about it. The Prophet Muhammad, peace and blessings be upon him, once described a man who did not perform his prayers as someone who was in the middle. If the issue is about faith then there are different consequences. Somebody offered his help when God's Messenger was preparing to go to battle. The Messenger of God asked him, "Do you believe?" When the man replied that he did not believe, the Messenger of God told him, "I do not need your help."[65]

---

[63] The direction in which a Muslim turns to when praying.
[64] *Sahih al-Buhari*, "Salah" 28; *Sunan at-Tirmidhi*, "Iman" 2; *Sunan an-Nasa'i*, "Iman" 9.
[65] *Sahih Muslim*, "Jihad" 150, *Sunan at-Tirmidhi*, "Siyar" 10.

In fact, faith is a boat that takes believers to a safe shore and prayer is its most vital element. As Alvarlı Efe stated, "Daily prayer is the main pillar of religion and its radiance. It is the moving force of the boat of religion, and the patriarch of all prayers."

The Messenger of God is reported to have made the following statement on a different occasion: "The most burdensome prayers for the hypocrites are night and dawn prayers."[66] Now we should ask ourselves if we are performing our prayers with enthusiasm. I feel that the name of the correct attitude to protect against a sense of hypocrisy is enthusiasm in prayer.

---

[66] *Sahih al-Buhari*, "Adhan" 34, "Mawakid" 20; *Sahih Muslim*, "Masajed" 252.

Chapter Six

# A COMPARISON BETWEEN QUR'ANIC AND NON-QUR'ANIC EDUCATION

# A COMPARISON BETWEEN QUR'ANIC AND NON-QUR'ANIC EDUCATION

In this chapter the issue of education is divided into two basic types: "Non-Qur'anic Education, Non-Qur'anic Morality, and Non-Qur'anic Method" and "Qur'anic Education, Qur'anic Morality, and Qur'anic Method."

This generation has a choice: to be insensitive, brutal, and cruel, letting ourselves be susceptible to the influence of extreme, distorted movements and philosophical views, or to be compassionate and far-sighted in the light of the superior principles of the Qur'an and its Divine orders.

In fact, whenever human beings have followed their baser selves and stayed away from the Qur'an they have become ruthless, cruel, brutal, and merciless towards those who are weak and helpless. They take advantage of the weak and powerless, exploiting them, looking down upon, and despising them. Whenever human beings have lost their power and become weak and powerless, they have also lost their honor and sacrificed their pride in return for small gains.

How does the Qur'an view humanity? How does it define and introduce the individual? What kind of person does the Qur'an desire people to become? While addressing these questions we will try to portray the type of person that the Qur'an describes as "Muslim." Then we will compile and discuss the principles pertaining to this issue. Afterwards, we will discuss how the individual who accepts and practices these principles is seen to be a true and complete Muslim, and how the society composed of such Muslims is an *ideal society.*

An individual may have two different statuses, one as a person and the second as a member of society. First of all, it is obvious that the happiness and safety of a society depends upon the happiness of the individual. An individual should have spiritual and material health and prosperity. The health and well being of people is measured by the strength of their faith, their willingness to perform good deeds and the conformity of their actions with religious principles.[67]

# 1. Non-Qur'anic Education

## a) Becoming a Pharaoh

Non-Qur'anic education, as we have seen up to the present day, turns individuals into potential Pharaohs, creating in them a feeling of contempt for others. From one point of view, a human being wishes to achieve power. In that case he or she becomes "aggressive, cruel, brutal, oppressive, and selfish." From another point of view, such a person is actually in a weak and powerless situation, making him or her destitute, pitiful, miserable and ready to grovel for favors. As Bediüzzaman explained, the one who is addicted to materialist philosophy is in fact a Pharaoh-like tyrant; he is a miserable Pharaoh who worships the most trivial things. Like the Devil, he is a stern person who kisses other people's feet in self-interest. As for the person who has received Qur'anic education, he is a servant who refuses to worship even the greatest of all creatures.[68]

Such a personality trait does not only belong to the Pharaoh who opposed Moses, but is also a common characteristic of all who resemble him throughout history. It seems that in this age there are more Pharaohs than at any other time. When such people need you or when their interests are at a stake, they bow and scrape before you; they prostrate before you and strive to get your help. Yet when these same people feel themselves to be in a safe, strong and powerful position, they then become aggressive, barbaric, and savage. The features that they share with the Pharaoh and with Nimrod come to the fore, making clear their "dual personalities."

The Qur'an portrays the twisted psychology of the Pharaoh as follows: *"Then he gathered (his men and hosts), and made a proclamation, saying: "I am your Supreme Lord!"* (An-Naziat 79:23–24)

---

[67] *cf.* Nursi. *Ibid.* p. 145.
[68] *Ibid.* p. 147.

This is what people say when they become a Pharaoh, seeing themselves as being the greatest, supported by their army and supporters.

There is also a moment and a situation when such people become miserable and pathetic. In this situation they are more wretched than the poorest of the poor and more contemptible than the lowest of all. The Qur'an portrays the psychology of such people who find themselves in such a state as follows:

> We brought the Children of Israel across the sea, and the Pharaoh and his hosts pursued them with vehement insolence and hostility, until (they were overwhelmed by the waters of the sea opened for Moses and his people to cross,) and when the drowning overtook the Pharaoh, he exclaimed: "I have come to believe that there is no deity save Him in whom the Children of Israel believe, and I am of the Muslims (those who have submitted themselves wholly to Him). (Yunus 10:90)

When what is said here is examined closely, it is easy to see that whatever is being said is no more than hypocritical cries and insincere words; it is clear that the Pharaoh is not genuine in his expressions, thoughts, and words. If he were actually expressing his true feelings in a state of righteousness at that moment, then the Almighty God would have accepted his faith. But, he prayed and turned to God insincerely because he had found himself in difficulty; this is why Almighty God did not accept his tragic cries. This type of behavior is a typical act of Pharaohs. You may come across hundreds of people like this in your life. They will come to your door and grovel in front of you asking for a promotion or a raise in salary. But when they get what they want, they disappear. They leave and condemn you to disloyalty of *"nasyan mansiyya."*[69] As a matter of fact it is easy to see that such people make no efforts to combat the problems concerning the nation, religion, faith, religious life or the education of children. It is painful to realize that they are trying to deceive you, and this leaves you with feelings of disgust.

It cannot be said that people who have not been exposed to a Qur'anic education are like a Pharaoh in every way. But it is possible that they may have a few of these negative traits. Taking this possibility into

---

[69] It means being a thing to be quite forgotten. This term is used in the Qur'an (Maryam 19:23).

account, we need to examine such cases carefully and confine ourselves to calling such behaviors "the morality of Pharaoh." Sometimes a believer (one who has faith) may also have aspects of the morality of Pharaoh while a non-believer can have the morality of Moses. If a believer continues to hold the morality of Pharaoh—may God protect us from this—it may consume the faithful and finally turn him or her into a Pharaoh. An unbeliever with the moral virtues of Moses, on the other hand, may finally achieve a higher status and be able to follow the path of Moses. As a matter of fact, God does not look at the external appearance, racial origin, or class origin of people; rather He looks into their hearts, their spiritual life, their piety, and religiosity. In short, He values a human being's quality and character.

God's Messenger is reported to have said the following concerning this matter: "Almighty God neither considers your physical appearance nor your face. He values your heart (the inner world) and your deeds."[70]

## b) How such Education Increases the Obstinacy of People and Acts as a Negative Factor

An individual who has received a non-Qur'anic education becomes stubborn and arrogant. Such people always put their pride, their honor, and their ego first. They disregard the numerous principles of humanity and violate many rights just to satisfy their own self, pride and honor. Our "sense of obstinacy" was instilled in us in order to help us to remain persistent and to not give up on a cause in which we believe.

In fact, Almighty God has strengthened us with a sense that is the starting point of what can be called persistency or stubbornness; this is so we do not give up on a cause that we have committed ourselves to, even if we become deprived of our property, our employment, or other blessings. However, if we abuse this sense of persistency and use it constantly to fight for unjust causes, then this feeling will be harmful. If such a tendency is continuous—may God protect us—it marks the beginning of our downfall. This type of person eventually drifts into the character of a Pharaoh. People with such a morality refuse to accept the "Truth,"

---

[70] *Sahih Muslim*, "Birr" 33; *Sunan ibn Majah*, "Zuhd" 9.

even when they come face to face with it and they do not refrain from groveling before others for the smallest favor.

From the past until today the situation has not changed. Whatever a non-Qur'anic education inculcates and produces in the human psyche today is the same as it did in the past. There are many Pharaohs today who speak of themselves as "we, the intellectuals" and despise all others, regarding those who do not agree with them as being lower than other humans. Such people become weak when they fall into a powerless state. There may be numerous Pharaoh-type people, people who when they achieve power and have an opportunity do not give others of different views the right to live. There is no difference between the characteristics of these contemporary Pharaohs and those of the past, except in context and peculiarities.

The main focus of non-Qur'anic education is feeding the stomach and satisfying the selfish/egoistic desires. When people who have had this kind of education think about the happiness of humankind, they think only of satisfying their ego and its desires.

It is thought by many that a number of countries have improved their economies and provided prosperity for their people, enabling them to achieve happiness. In their view, the ideal world is to be established as described by utopian authors. Genuine peace and happiness can be found in faith and submission to God however, they see happiness as a result of material prosperity, having attributed peace and happiness to the perfection of economic conditions and to the solution of all economic problems. For such non-believers, if a state is all powerful and if their pockets are full, then this means that society is at peace.

However, the escalating suicide-rate, the emergence of crises, the rapid change in fashion, and people's attempt to satisfy themselves with various pseudo-religions and/or thought-systems are all indications of a serious dissatisfaction and restlessness in society, indicating that material prosperity is not enough to ensure genuine and lasting happiness. We can call such an occurrence the "philosophy of consolation." Those who adhere to this philosophy are happy and content if they eat well and are satisfied materially. As a matter of fact, this is a philosophy that sees the main goal of humans as being the feeding of the stomach and the satisfaction of egoistical desires.

## c) The aim of Non-Qur'anic Education

The aim of non-Qur'anic education is profit. The basis of such struggles is nothing more than making money. Upon the completion of a task, it is people who are outside "the faith frame" that ask the following, "What's in it for me?"

Since such people view everything from a materialist perspective, they ask: "Did this country get to the place it is today because of your prayers? Did society achieve happiness because you're fasting?" In fact, people with this mindset will never understand those who speak on behalf of justice and truth and who defend the faith and the Qur'an. Such a trend may be defined as "the vulgarity of a non-Qur'anic attitude."

## d) Non-Qur'anic Education Depends on Struggle, Dialectics, and Demagogy

"Seeking self-interest causes battles over material resources, and conflict brings strife."[71] A society whose sole aim is to achieve personal interests may lead to never-ending conflicts and continuing battles within the society as the stakes available cannot satisfy all desires. All the "ism's", from capitalism to communism and from socialism to fascism are waging a war to gain the stakes in this framework. Moreover, according to such a mentality, acts such as the occupation of another's country and finding a means to confiscate all the property of the conquered are justified by the ends. In fact, survival in non-Qur'anic systems is based on interest or gain. The most important motto for such people is to fight and eliminate the weak. In such systems, might is right; life is the privilege of the powerful.

For those who adhere to such unfounded principles, powerful and victorious nations will be the survivors of the competition between nations and states. This understanding, which regards the relations between animals and plants as nothing more than struggle and warfare, which sees "life as consisting of struggle," considers the current situation of human beings to be the result of war and the extermination of human beings by one another in the search for legitimacy.

---

[71] Nursi, *Ibid*. p.147.

## e) Relations among Societies Based on Racism and Chauvinism

According to non-Qur'anic education, the most important relations among individuals and nations are based upon a vulgar racism and sometimes—as we can witness today—these relations depend upon ideas found in socialism and communism, that is, they are based on the idea of sharing. These ideologies aim to unify society within these bonds. In fact, racism, chauvinism, and similar ideologies have been designed to absorb other ideologies; thus they are each following a policy that will help to reach their goals. For example, communism was programmed to consume and wipe out all opposing systems. Moreover, as history has shown us, fascism and Nazism were also designed to survive by destroying all opposing systems. As a matter of fact, the consequences of an education based on non-Qur'anic enculturation and the pains inflicted by it were made evident during the first and second World Wars.

## f) Non-Qur'anic Education Takes Force as Its Cornerstone

Social, philosophical, and educational systems that are not based on the Truth are based on power. Might is right; this is no more than the morality of a Pharaoh. Power which does not respect human values will violate human rights. A person who deals with a problem on the principle of force and who attributes everything to power can hardly avoid committing such violations. Humanity has witnessed numerous examples of this, especially in the twentieth century. This has been true to the extent that, over and above the aggression displayed by individuals, societies have begun to act with an instinct for destruction and for the elimination of all else. As a result of such destruction, caused by the non-Qur'anic education instilled in human hearts, a number of problems have started to emerge in Muslim societies; it is as if they have been polluted by radioactive wastes of such education.

## 2. Qur'anic Education

### a) The Disciple of the Qur'an Is a Servant

A disciple of the Qur'an cannot become a brutal, cruel, oppressive tyrant nor be a draconic person in any way. Rather such a person is merely a servant; a servant of God. The Qur'an reminds us constantly that human beings are the servants of Almighty God and emphasizes that this status is an honor and a reward for us. If, due to a Qur'anic education, a human being realizes that he or she is the servant of Almighty God, then this person has achieved the highest virtue. The most distinguished characteristic of God's Messenger is the fact that he was a servant of God. The Prophet Muhammad was His Messenger and His servant. The Prophet Muhammad, peace and blessings be upon him, was a servant of God before he became a Messenger. After his death his Prophethood ended, yet he is still the dearest, the most dignified and the most gracious of servants. Even if everything else ends, servitude to God will continue forever. As a matter of fact, everything comes to an end, including the Prophethood, guardianship and all duties attached to such. There is only one everlasting thing: servitude to the eternal God.

In response to God's command to humanity, *"Now O humankind! Worship your Lord..."* (Al-Baqara 2:21), a faithful person comes before God forty times a day with a sense of servitude and says, *"You alone do We worship, and from You alone do we seek help."* (Al-Fatiha 1:5)

Good Muslims are glorious servants who distain to worship even the greatest of all creatures. They are servants and slaves only to God. If they possess such a characteristic then they are regarded as real sultans, even if they may appear to be humiliated. They will never bow or surrender before a Pharaoh. The Prophet's life is full of wonderful examples of such behavior. His Companions never were servants to other people, even under coercion.

If you could imagine yourself living in the age of the Prophet Muhammad, peace and blessings be upon him, you would see the torturing, beating and burning of Ammar ibn Yasir, Mus'ab ibn Umayr, Sa'd ibn Abi Waqqas and you would be surprised by their deeply rooted commitment to be true servants of God. In the following periods one can also find similar personalities, albeit all with different depths of commitment and persistence. As a matter of fact, there have been numerous people who were servants of God in every age; they all opposed injustice, raised their voices because they were concerned with justice, defended, and established justice, destroying oppression and disbelief. They took the Qur'an as their guide and they lived for its ideals.

There are some tasks that are easy to accomplish. Establishing community associations, forming groups, organizing congresses, working for money, fees or for other rewards are undemanding transactions. What is important is to raise a generation who will constantly defend and establish justice without material or religious expectations. This generation will seek only to be servants of God; servitude to Him will be all they seek. Their most spectacular title will be the discipleship of the Qur'an. They will not dream of being called by any other title than this.

### b) They are Humble and Modest towards God

A disciple of the Qur'an is a humble person. The external appearance of such people may give the impression that they are lazy and inactive. This is wrong; such people are tranquil, yet able to overcome everything as they are so committed and decisive in not bowing down before anyone except their Creator. They consider such an act as polytheism. The disciples of the Qur'an seem to be weak and poor from the outside. This is one of their distinct characteristics. Their weaknesses and poverties are wings that elevate them to God. The more they are aware of their unlimited powerlessness and infinite need in their heart, the more they put their trust in God. They in fact have a very strong inner dynamism.

God's Messenger is reported to have appealed to Him as follows: "Do not leave us alone with our ego, even for the blink of an eye."[72] The weakness, poverty, and modesty are spiritual wings that take people to the higher echelons of spirituality; this happens as people become aware of this weakness and poverty in their selves and in their search for the gratification of God.

### c) Their Aim Is to Attain God's Appreciation

The aim of disciples of the Qur'an and the dreams they cherish are to achieve the commendation of God alone. They always look for the appreciation of God and they expect to hear the following address, "(... to the righteous God will say:) 'O, you soul at rest (content with the truths of faith and God's commands, and with His treatment of His creatures)!'" (Al-Facr 89:27)

---

[72] *Sunan Abu Dawud*, "Adab" 101; *Musnad*, 5/42.

Prophet Joseph, peace be upon him, describes this ideal horizon as follows:

> My Lord! You have indeed granted me some important part of the rule and imparted to me some knowledge of the inner meaning of all happenings (including dreams). O You, Originator of the heavens and the earth, each with particular features! You are my Owner and Guardian in this world and in the Hereafter. Take my soul to You as a Muslim, and join me with the righteous. (Yusuf 12:101).

Prophet Joseph refused a high status in Egypt and became weakened after many years of suffering and crying. His father had run out of tears in his grief. His brothers, who had treated him badly, later followed his path. It is important to think over this appeal carefully, an appeal which he made while he in the mental and spiritual state of being before God.

All these examples show that there is a profit much more valuable than material prosperity, worldly happiness or any other sort of comfort which satisfies the heart; the appreciation and commendation of God.

The goal of any effort made by a believer is to gain Divine appreciation, i.e. to please God. Such people pray to God with a hope of earning His blessings; this is what He has ordered to be done. Believers assume that they will attain their rewards in return for good deeds in the Hereafter. When they receive a favor or encounter a blessing in this world, they are thankful for it. They prostrate before God. In fact, the faithful are preoccupied only with the idea of gaining Divine commendation. The Qur'an confirms this in many verses; some examples are as follows:

> Say: "I am commanded to worship God, sincere in faith in Him and practicing the Religion purely for His sake." (Az-Zumar 39:11)

> Say: "I worship God, sincere in my faith in Him and practicing the Religion purely for His sake." (Az-Zumar 39:14)

Human beings are encouraged to devotion and to seek God's commendation in the following verses:

> They were not enjoined anything other than that they should worship God, sincere in faith in Him and practicing the Religion purely for His sake, as people of pure faith; and establish the Prayer in accordance with its conditions; and pay the Prescribed Purifying Alms. And that is the upright, ever-true Religion. (Al-Baiyyinah 98:5)

## d) Their Life Motto Is Cooperation

The Qur'an views cooperation and solidarity as the basic principles of life. This view can be found in the following verse:

> ... help one another in virtue and goodness, and righteousness and piety, and do not help one another in sinful, iniquitous acts and hostility; (in all your actions) keep from disobedience to God in reverence for Him and piety. Surely God is severe in retribution. (Al-Ma'idah 5:2)

Thus, Muslims should help one another to perform what is prescribed or to avoid what is prohibited by their religion. They should try to practice their religion in solidarity and cooperation with one another. We should not forget that the social dimension of Islam is the more significant aspect. Therefore, it is essential to improve this aspect, as recommended in the following verse: *"... help one another in virtue and goodness, and righteousness and piety..."* (Al-Ma'idah 5:2)

Life in nature does not consist of struggles; rather it consists of cooperation and solidarity. Molecules help plants, plants help animals, and animals rush to our help. Cooperation can be found in everything. The particles, atoms, and molecules all continue their existence as part of a cycle of cooperation.

The faithful view the universe as a unity and harmony of such cooperation and say that "throughout the universe there is cooperation." Therefore, human beings should conform to this general harmony found throughout the universe and run to the assistance of others in order to preserve this harmony and musical symphony.

## e) The Bond among Us Is That of Brother and Sisterhood

The Qur'an equates the bonding among the faithful to the relationship of siblings. A relationship should be established among all Muslims and the sense of being siblings should be emphasized once more in the light of such bonding. People of the same faith, i.e. those who practice Islam, should cling together, becoming inseparable. As the Qur'an points out, *"The believers are but brothers"* (Al-Hujurat 49:10). A believer should regard every other faithful person as a sibling and should see the universe as "the center of brother and sisterhood."

## f) The Idea of Justice Is Central

Qur'anic education accepts "justice" as the source of support rather than "force." Qur'anic education postulates that "whoever is just is powerful." A faithful person lives in the belief that with the help and support of God justice will prevail in the future, even if at the moment that person lives in a state of weakness.

For a Muslim, respecting justice is in fact a form of prayer. Caliph Umar set an excellent example of this in the following event. It is narrated that a non-Muslim and Caliph Umar had a problem that was taken to court to settle. The judge summoned Caliph Umar, the leader of the Muslim community, to the court. He came to the court and called upon the judge to establish justice.

A believer who has not been influenced by non-Qur'anic philosophical systems always practices and lives in justice and recommends the same, as seen in the following verse in the Qur'an:

> By Time (especially the last part of it, heavy with events), most certainly, human is in loss, except those who believe and do good, righteous deeds, and exhort one another to truth, and exhort one another to steadfast patience (in the face of misfortunes, and suffering in God's way, and in doing good deeds, and not committing sins). (Al-Asr 103:1–3)

The Turkish poet Mehmet Akif wrote the following verses to emphasize the importance of the concept of justice:

> *The Creator has endless names, starting with the Just*
> *For a servant it is such a glorious thing to hold and raise justice*
> *Why do they read the chapter "Al-Asr"*
> *When the respected Companions leave a gathering?*
>
> *Because there is the secret of salvation in this chapter*
> *First comes the reality of justice, second comes salvation*
> *Then follows The Just, and then comes persistence, O humankind!*
> *When these four come together and unite, there will be no downfall for you...*[73]

People are able to survive with justice. If there is a hidden truth in things, then it is based on God's attribute of justice. In fact, the title of *The Just* is one of the greatest attributes of God. A believer attributes

---

[73] Ersoy, *Ibid.,* (vol. 6, p. 403).

power to justice. Whoever is just, he is powerful. The following is an Islamic principle: "Justice is exalted and honorable and rights cannot be abandoned." Therefore, justice is always supreme and nothing will stand in its way.

# INDEX